Informal Assessments for Transition Planning

Gary M. Clark,
James R. Patton,
and
L. Rozelle Moulton

pro·ed
An International Publisher

8700 Shoal Creek Boulevard
Austin, Texas 78757-6897
800/897-3202   Fax 800/397-7633
Order online at http://www.proedinc.com

© 2000 by PRO-ED, Inc.
8700 Shoal Creek Boulevard
Austin, Texas 78757-6897
800/897-3202   Fax 800/397-7633
Order online at http://www.proedinc.com

Library of Congress Cataloging-in-Publication Data

Clark, Gary M.
    Informal assessments for transition planning / Gary M. Clark, James R. Patton, L.
Rozelle Moulton.
    p.   cm.
Includes bibliographical references.
    ISBN-13: 978-089079740-2
    ISBN-10: 0-89079-849-4 (softcover : alk. paper)
    1. Handicapped youth—Education (Secondary)   2. School-to-work transition.   3.
Vocational guidance for the handicapped.   4. Educational tests and measurements.   I.
Patton, James R.   II. Moulton, L. Rozelle.   III. Title.

LC3969 .C5   2000
371.9'0473—dc21   99-086984
                                                                              CIP

This book is designed in Cheltenham and Frutiger.

Printed in the United States of America

    8   9   10   09   08   07   06

Contents

Section 1
Introduction

The purpose of transition planning is to put into effect a plan of action, prior to a student's exit from school, that ensures a seamless movement from school to various postsecondary settings. For this to occur, three key elements need to be in place. First, comprehensive planning that includes assessing needs and developing individual plans has to be conducted. Second, the individual plan must be carried out. Lastly, ongoing coordination between school and postsecondary agencies, service providers, and other settings is essential. This coordination from the community sector can range from sharing information to extensive engagement in the transition planning process of a student.

The intent of transition assessment is to gather information in an organized fashion that will be useful for developing appropriate transition plans. In our opinion, transition planning typically includes the generation of two types of goals: instructional goals and linkage goals. To serve students with disabilities well, transition assessment should be comprehensive and responsive to a student's interests and preferences. All major areas of adult functioning, not just employment outcomes, should be considered. For many students, only a few areas of transition need will be identified; for others, needs will be expansive.

The basic tenets on which sound transition assessment practices should be assessed are as follows:

- The more known about receiving settings along with the student's competence to deal with these settings, the more likely the student's chances for making a successful transition.

- The more comprehensive the assessment of transition needs, the easier (i.e., straightforward) the task of developing useful and appropriate transition plans.

- The more the school-based professionals are involved in the transition process, the more likely they are to understand and be able to address a student's needs. (Patton & Dunn, 1998, p. 21)

The primary purpose of *Informal Assessments for Transition Planning* is to provide a comprehensive source of assessment procedures so that practitioners can identify the transition needs of students. It is used most effectively in conjunction with the *Transition Planning Inventory* (TPI; Clark & Patton, 1997). However, it can be used by itself as a means of generating useful information on students' transition needs. Our belief is that the TPI and this resource

1

form a package of assessment techniques that is self-contained—a form of one-stop shopping so to speak.

This opening section is made up of two sub-sections. The first part provides background information related to the transition assessment and planning process along with a description of the TPI. The second part describes the components of this book.

Background Information

This section briefly highlights the major elements of the transition planning process, with special attention given to the assessment of transition needs. An overview (purpose, development, and components) of the TPI is also provided. This overview is especially important for those using this book as a stand-alone material, in order to provide a basic understanding of the TPI, as it is referred to frequently.

Transition Planning Areas

Even though no set of transition planning domains has been agreed upon, a common core of transition areas can be identified as important when thinking about the transition from school to postschool settings. Based on information from 17 states, Clark and Patton (1997) found the following domains (listed alphabetically) being used by more than 50% of the states analyzed:

- Community participation
- Daily living
- Employment
- Financial/income management
- Health
- Independent living (includes living arrangements)
- Leisure/recreation
- Postsecondary education
- Relationships/social skills
- Transportation/mobility
- Vocational training

As one might conclude, some degree of inter-state variation and professional discretion exists, so that actual domains used by different sources are likely to be different. For example, the TPI uses nine domains, two of which are not on this list.

Transition Assessment and Planning Process

Although the process of identifying transition needs and generating transition plans based on these needs is a relatively simple idea to consider on a general level, the process is actually a complex one that requires a framework. Figure 1 illustrates the fundamental elements of this process. As can be seen in the figure, two outcomes of initial assessment are possible: (1) the immediate generation of transition-related goals and (2) the need for more in-depth information. Both of these outcomes are discussed in the following passages.

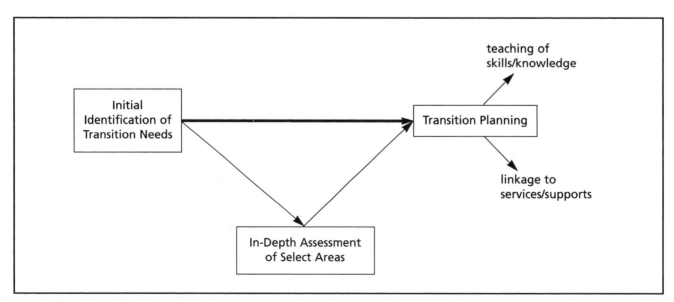

Figure 1. Transition planning process. *Note.* From *Transition Planning Inventory* (p. 26), by G. M. Clark and J. R. Patton, 1997, Austin, TX: PRO-ED. Copyright 1997 by PRO-ED, Inc. Reprinted with permission.

Two different categories of goals are possible. The first category refers to instructional goals that focus on skill development and concept/knowledge acquisition and that lead to planned instructional activities. The other category of goals relates to any number of linkage goals that are identified to connect students and their families to supports and/or services that will be needed prior to or after school completion.

An important point needs to be emphasized in regard to this process. Not all transition planning domains will be problematic for most students with disabilities. However, most students, disabled or not, are likely to have some transition needs. Sometimes it will be important to clarify those needs that are identified initially by conducting more in-depth levels of assessment.

Need for In-Depth Assessment

The nature of a transition needs assessment is to identify areas where planning and action (instruction and linkage) should occur. The reality of current school settings requires that this mandated transition planning process be relatively easy to implement. As a result, an initial transition needs assessment must generate information in an effective and efficient (i.e., not time-consuming and not complicated) manner. Instruments like the *Transition Planning Inventory* have been designed with these factors in mind. Nevertheless, there is a price to pay for ease of use, and that price in regard to transition assessment is lack of depth. As a result, when using an instrument such as the TPI, sometimes practitioners will need to obtain more detailed information.

Additional information that contributes to understanding a student's transition needs can be generated from a number of sources. An array of exiting data that can be extremely useful for elaborating on specific needs may already exist. For example, adaptive behavior measures, if the data are current, yield information that relates very nicely to transition planning. Other sources of existing information are listed in Table 1 as well as in the TPI manual and Clark's (1998) *Assessment for Transition Planning*.

Other sources of more in-depth information include the many informal inventories that have been developed by individuals or school districts throughout the country. Some of these are provided in Section 3 of this book.

Certain commercially available instruments may also provide helpful information for completing the transition needs picture. A list of these instruments is found in Table 1. More detailed descriptions of these transition-specific measures can also be found in the TPI manual or in Clark (1998).

Transition Planning Inventory

Although this book can be used by itself for generating transition needs information, it can also be used with the TPI. The close relationship between this book and the TPI is obvious, as the expanded items contained in Section 2 of this book are based on the transition domains and transition planning statements used in the TPI. This section concentrates on basic information about the TPI and, accordingly, is written primarily for those who are not using the TPI for identifying transition needs.

Purpose. The TPI is designed to provide school personnel with a systematic way to address critical transition planning areas, as mandated by the Individuals with Disabilities Education Act (IDEA) of 1990 and its reauthorization in 1997. It emphasizes basing transition assessment and planning on the individual student's needs, preferences, and interests. The instrument requests information about perceived transition needs from the student, parents/ guardians, and school-based personnel. The student forms and home forms can be administered individually or in group format. The data collected are profiled for use during transition planning meetings. The TPI can often lead directly to the generation of instructional and linkage goals.

Development. The TPI was developed in the mid-1990s to provide a framework for comprehensively assessing transition needs. The original draft version contained over 600 items, but was reduced to the current 46 items after considering the practical realities, mentioned previously, and the completion of field testing. Studies were performed on the TPI to establish its validity and reliability.

Components. The TPI kit is composed of a number of items. The major components of the TPI are the following:

- *Student, Home, and School Forms*—these are separate forms that are completed by indicated persons. The Student Form includes 15 open-ended statements that focus on determining the student's preferences and interests. A Spanish version of the Home Form is available.
- *Profile and Further Assessment Recommendations Form*—all collected data are recorded on this form. A space for organizing further assessment activities is included on this form.

TABLE 1

Commercially Available Tests and Procedures for Assessing Transition Needs

General Category	Selected Types of Measures	Specific Example(s)
Nonspecific to transition	Achievement tests	Adult Basic Learning Examination–Second Edition (Karlsen & Gardner, 1986)
	Adaptive behavior measures	AAMR Adaptive Behavior Scales–School, Second Edition (Lambert, Nihira, & Leland, 1993)
	Aptitude tests	Differential Aptitude Test, Fifth Edition (Bennett, Seashore, & Wesman, 1990)
	Communication tests	Communicative Abilities in Daily Living (Holland, 1980)
	Learning styles	Learning Styles Inventory (Dunn, Dunn, & Price, 1995)
	Manual dexterity	Crawford Small Parts Dexterity Test (Crawford, 1981)
	Occupational interest	Occupational Aptitude Survey and Interest Schedule–2 (Parker, 1991)
	Personality/social skills	Basic Personality Inventory (Jackson, 1995)
Specific to transition	Needs assessment	Transition Planning Inventory (Clark & Patton, 1997)
		Enderle–Severson Transition Rating Scale–Revised (Enderle & Severson, 1997)
	Life skills	BRIGANCE Life Skills Inventory (Brigance, 1995)
		LCCE Knowledge and Performance Battery (Brolin, 1992)
		Tests for Everyday Living (Halpern, Irvin, & Landman, 1979)
	Self-determination	Arc's Self-Determination Scale
	Quality of life	Quality of Life Questionnaire (Schalock & Keith, 1993)
		Quality of Student Life Questionnaire (Keith & Schalock, 1995)
	Work-related behavior	Transition Behavior Scale (McCarney, 1989)
	Social	Social and Prevocational Information Battery–Revised (Halpern, Irvin, & Munkres, 1986)

Note. From *Transition from School to Young Adulthood: Basic Concepts and Recommended Practices,* (p. 24), by J. R. Patton and C. Dunn, 1998, Austin, TX: PRO-ED. Copyright 1998 by PRO-ED. Reprinted with permission.

- *Administration and Resource Guide*—contains overview of the instrument, background information, directions for various administrations, guidelines for interpreting and using the results (includes three extensive case studies), information regarding the technical features of the instrument, and seven useful appendixes.

- *Informal Assessments for Transition Planning* (this book).

Teacher Feedback. Based on the feedback of professionals in many states, a Spanish version of the TPI Home Form was developed in 1998. The rationale for producing this form is that a significant number of the parents/guardians of students with disabilities are not native English speakers. Because this process is so important to families, having information available in Spanish was warranted.

The development of this book was also sparked by the requests of those involved with transition duties in the schools. Many people have been pleased with the TPI; however, most did not have easy access to other techniques that were practical for generating more in-depth information in various transition planning areas. This book was written in response to this need.

Components of *Informal Assessments for Transition Planning*

This book is composed of two major types of informal assessments. The first type, referred to as "Comprehensive Informal Inventory of Knowledge and Skills for Transition," is provided in Section 2 of the book. The other type of assessment, referred to as "Selected Informal Assessment Instruments for Transition," is found in Section 3.

Comprehensive Informal Inventory of Knowledge and Skills for Transition

Section 2 contains a listing of 634 items. It represents an expansion of the original 46 items used in the TPI. The 46 competency items are broken down into more specific subcompetency statements. This extensive listing of statements allows the transition specialist to obtain a more complete picture of a competency when a more elaborate sense of the present level of performance is needed.

Due to the vast number of items, only in exceptional situations would it be desirable to administer all of them; however, certain items or sections could be selected for use, depending on the generally recognized needs of the student. Individualized assessment techniques could be developed based on this expansive listing.

If used in conjunction with the TPI, this section acts as a Level 2 type of assessment, with the TPI being the Level 1 assessment. In this arrangement, the TPI would be administered first, with the selection of certain items from the Level 2 items when more in-depth information was needed. A more detailed explanation of this procedure is presented at the beginning of Section 2.

Selected Informal Assessment Instruments for Transition

Section 3 of this book provides 45 informal instruments that have come to our attention and for which permission has been granted to use in this book. The instruments are listed according the the nine major transition planning domains used in the TPI: employment, further education/training, daily living, leisure activities, community participation, health, self-determination, communication, and interpersonal relationships. A list of all the instruments included here and organized by transition domain can be found at the beginning of Section 3 (pp. 45–46). Each instrument is coded according to who (teacher, parent/guardian, student) should complete it.

The instruments in Section 3 were selected in a somewhat arbitrary fashion. Over the years, we have come to know these instruments. These instruments were included in this resource based on a certain level of appeal to us. We do not mean to imply that this is an exhaustive list or that these instruments represent the best that are available. They merely are offered as informal instruments that practitioners may find useful. We readily admit that we probably missed some excellent instruments. We also would have included other excellent instruments had we been able to obtain permission.

If this book is used with the TPI, Section 3 can be considered a Level 3 assessment in that it provides some wonderful additional techniques for acquiring a detailed picture of student needs. Certain instruments in Section 3 can enhance significantly the amount of information about certain transition competencies. A summary of the levels of assessment associated with using the TPI and this book is provided in Table 2.

TABLE 2
Three Levels of Assessment Using the TPI
and *Informal Assessments for Transition Planning*

Level 1	**Administration of TPI—all three forms**
	Provides an initial, efficient identification and screening of major transition planning area needs.
Level 2	**Selection of appropriate items from Section 2 of *Informal Assessments for Transition Planning***
	Provides a comprehensive inventory of transition planning needs or the basis for selective in-depth assessment in one or more transition planning areas.
Level 3	**Administration of selected informal inventories from Section 3 of *Informal Assessments for Transition Planning*—when needed**
	Provides a collection of informal instruments or procedures for selective in-depth assessment.

Additional Thoughts

Informal Assessments for Transition Planning has been designed so that practitioners can pick it up and use it immediately. The intuitive nature of this material addresses the ease-of-use criterion that transition professionals require. In addition to the clear instructions on how to use the materials in Sections 2 and 3, we also have included two additional features that merit attention at this point.

First, we have provided a sample form that can be used for the generation of a statement of transi-

tion needs. This Statement of Transition Needs form is located in Appendix A. Second, we have included a case study that shows a sampling of the three levels of assessment possible when using the TPI and this book. The case study clearly shows how the various levels relate to each other. This case study is found in Appendix B.

We continue to strive to provide ways to assess comprehensively the needs of some students in ways that practitioners will find useful to students, desirable, and practical. We hope that this book contributes to this goal.

Section 2

Comprehensive Informal Inventory of Knowledge and Skills for Transition

In this section, we list more detailed transition statements designed to be used as a more comprehensive inventory for transition planning. The numbered items, which are primary components of the Comprehensive Informal Inventory, reflect each major planning area and correspond to the 46 items on the *Transition Planning Inventory* (TPI). The statements, elaborating specific areas of knowledge or skills under each of the 46 TPI items, provide more in-depth assessment for each of the TPI items. The statements are written to reflect the potential needs of a wide variety of types and levels of severity among disabilities and needed functional skills. Because of the unique and varied needs of such a range of students, some statements will be too narrow and others will be too broad.

No individual should expect to be proficient in all of the statement areas. Nor is it reasonable to expect all students to be able to perform all statement areas independently. Some students will always need some type of support in the living, employment, and social aspects of their lives. Inherent in evaluating a student's independence is not only whether the student is able to complete the task without assistance, but also whether the student is able to complete the task spontaneously without being told.

The wording of the statements contained in this section may also be revised and used as potential goal statements in assisting a student to maximize his or her independence. Goal statements should include a statement of the target area and an inherent end point; that is, an evaluator or parent should be able to measure when the goal has been completed. Then goals may be subdivided into more specific measurable objectives or units. Each goal statement should be assumed to follow a stem that identifies the student (e.g., "Mary will be able to demonstrate how to . . ."). See Appendix E of the TPI for a set of goal statements for most of the statement areas in this Comprehensive Informal Inventory of Knowledge and Skills for Transition.

The transition knowledge or skill statements are not written in any purposeful sequence. Likewise, each area is not exclusive unto itself for the purpose of developing goal statements from this inventory. It is quite likely that a student may use both a statement from *Manages own money* (Item 15) that focuses on developing a budget, and a statement that addresses using the budget listed under *Knows how to locate a place to live in the community* (Item 12). When considering whether to include a goal, or when evaluating whether a goal has been accomplished, each goal also should be evaluated for the independence, efficiency, and confidence with which it has been completed.

For the purpose of developing goal statements, the statements here are not intended to be a final or definitive listing of all possible areas of transition knowledge and skills. They are intended to spark ideas in the minds of parents, students, and other team members as to a student's present level of performance in transition knowledge and skills. This listing is not intended to be a scope and sequence chart or a curriculum. School-based professionals should modify, sequence, and/or link the statements to specific environments to reflect the unique needs of each student.

Directions for Level 2 Assessment in Transition Planning

The following are three basic ways to use the Comprehensive Informal Inventory of Knowledge and Skills for Transition:

1. A follow-up assessment for planning areas on the TPI that indicates a need for further assessment or more in-depth assessment.

2. An initial screening in *selected* transition knowledge and skill areas that provides an Individualized Education Program (IEP) team with specific knowledge or skills information that might indicate a need for IEP goals or objectives.

3. A comprehensive initial screening of a student for determining specific IEP transition service needs for knowledge or skills (ages 14–15) and suggested specific needed transition services (ages 16 and older, or younger when appropriate).

Each of these approaches to using the Comprehensive Informal Inventory is discussed in the following sections, with suggested directions for administration.

Option 1: Follow-Up Assessment to the TPI

Any item on the TPI Profile and Further Assessment Recommendations Form that reflects a need for more detailed information, some uncertainty, or lack of information by respondents about a student's knowledge or skill is an item that needs further assessment. In the case of a TPI administration with *three*

respondents (student, parent/guardian, and school representative), such an item could show (a) two or more "Don't Know" (DK) responses, (b) one DK response and widely discrepant ratings by the other two respondents, or (c) simply an expressed need for more specific information even though the item was rated with some agreement. In an administration of the TPI where only *one* or *two* response forms are completed, an item in question would be one that has a response of DK, or, in the case of two respondents, demonstrates disagreement as to whether the student has or does not have the knowledge or skill being rated.

For example, let's say that Item 3 (*Knows how to get a job*) on the TPI Profile and Further Assessment Recommendations Form shows that the Home rating was DK and the School and Student ratings were 1 and 5, respectively. In this example, it is clear that there is a high degree of disagreement about whether or not the student knows how to get a job, uncertainty as to all the aspects involved in knowing how to get a job, and thus uncertainty about whether or not the student knows how to do the various tasks involved with getting a job. In this case, the indication on the TPI Profile and Further Assessment Recommendations Form is for further assessment for Item 3. Item 3 of the Comprehensive Informal Inventory addresses 15 specific component knowledge or skill areas of what is involved in knowing how to get a job. Each of the 15 component knowledge or skill areas in the inventory for TPI Item 3 is presented as a way to focus on the specifics, rather than a summary or general assessment, of knowing how to get a job.

Students, parents/guardians, or school personnel may complete the Comprehensive Informal Inventory independently or together. We recommend a joint completion of the instrument in order to arrive at an initial consensus on what a student knows or can do.

Directions: Select the TPI item(s) from the TPI Profile and Further Assessment Recommendations Form indicating a need for further assessment. Go to the same numbered item(s) on the Comprehensive Informal Inventory form. You may respond to *all* knowledge or skill statements, or respond *selectively* to those you believe are appropriate for the student.

You have two response options for each statement. First, you may indicate whether or not the specific knowledge or skill area is one that is appropriate for addressing on the IEP or Individualized Transition Plan (ITP) with a goal or objective by putting a check (✔) or an X by the item in the column titled "Goals/Objectives Needed." The other response option is to indicate that there is a question as to whether the student has the knowledge or skill and further in-depth assessment is recommended. Again, respond by putting a check (✔) or an X by the item under the column titled "Further Assessment Needed." Any additional comments can be written in the "Notes" column.

Estimated time for completion: 3 to 4 minutes per knowledge or skill area.

Option 2: Initial Screening in Selected Transition Knowledge and Skill Areas

The Comprehensive Informal Inventory covers the 46 knowledge or skill areas used in the TPI. Under each of the 46 areas are a number of specific knowledge or skill statements that indicate subskills that lead to successful performance of each area. Not all students need a comprehensive assessment for transition planning, but some areas of knowledge and skill may be obvious from observations and stated preferences and interests by the students. Moving directly to these selected areas for in-depth screening with this inventory may be helpful.

For example, a student has stated an interest in going to college after high school, has indicated frustration in not having made a choice in some occupational area, has some continuing problems with managing her health needs, and feels that she has little control in determining choices in her life. For this student, it would be appropriate to use the following items of the Comprehensive Informal Inventory:

Item 2: Makes informed choices among occupational alternatives, based on his or her own interests, preferences, and abilities.

Item 9: Knows how to gain entry into an appropriate college or university.

Item 10: Can succeed in an appropriate postsecondary program.

Item 26: Maintains good physical health.

Item 27: Addresses physical problems that arise.

Item 35: Sets personal goals.

Item 36: Makes personal decisions.

Students, parents/guardians, or school personnel may complete the inventory independently or together. We recommend a joint completion of the instrument in order to arrive at an initial consensus on what a student knows or can do.

Directions: Select the knowledge and skill areas of interest for in-depth screening with the Compre-

hensive Informal Inventory. You may respond to *all* knowledge or skill statements in an area or respond *selectively* to those you believe are appropriate for the student.

You have two response options for each statement. First, you may indicate whether or not the specific knowledge or skill area is one that is appropriate for addressing on the IEP or ITP with a goal or objective by putting a check (✔) or an X by the item in the column titled "Goals/Objectives Needed." The other response option is to indicate that there is a question as to whether the student has the knowledge or skill and further in-depth assessment is recommended. Again, respond by putting a check (✔) or an X by the item under the column titled "Further Assessment Needed." Any additional comments can be written in the "Notes" column.

Estimated time for completion: 3 to 4 minutes per knowledge or skill area.

Option 3: Comprehensive Initial Screening for Transition Planning

One of the planned features of the TPI and other inventories like it is to cover as many transition planning areas as possible in an efficient format. The TPI has 46 competency items across 9 transition planning domains. It was important to provide an instrument that could be administered in approximately 15 to 20 minutes to keep assessment time reasonable. This is easy to do for students with whom school personnel are already familiar and who may have only a few transition service needs.

New students or students who are difficult to evaluate may need a more comprehensive screening in determining the present level of performance for transition planning in the IEP or ITP. The Comprehensive Informal Inventory is expansive in its scope of coverage (9 domains, 46 competency items, and over 600 knowledge and skill statements). The inventory can provide an excellent baseline for identifying initial transition planning needs and areas where further assessment is needed.

Students, parents/guardians, or school personnel may complete the inventory independently or together. We recommend a joint completion of the instrument in order to arrive at an initial consensus on what a student knows or can do. Due to its length, respondents have the option to divide the inventory into sections and complete them at different times to avoid fatigue.

Directions: You may respond to *all* knowledge or skill statements in every area, or respond *selectively* within each of the areas to those statements you believe are appropriate for the student.

You have two response options for each statement. First, you may indicate whether or not the specific knowledge or skill area is one that is appropriate for addressing on the IEP or ITP with a goal or objective by putting a check (✔) or an X by the item in the column titled "Goals/Objectives Needed." The other response option is to indicate that there is a question as to whether the student has the knowledge or skill and further in-depth assessment is recommended. Again, respond by putting a check (✔) or an X by the item under the column titled "Further Assessment Needed." Any additional comments can be written in the "Notes" column.

Estimated time for completion: 3 to 4 minutes per knowledge or skill area; approximately 2 hours for all statements in all areas.

Note: Permission is granted to the user to make unlimited copies of sections of the "Comprehensive Informal Inventory of Knowledge and Skills for Transition" for teaching or clinical purposes.

Comprehensive Informal Inventory of Knowledge and Skills for Transition

Goals/ Objectives Needed	Further Assessment Needed	Transition Knowledge and Skill Statements	Notes
EMPLOYMENT			
		1. **Knows the requirements and demands of his or her preferred occupations.**	
☐	☐	Knows how to seek others employed in preferred occupation to learn about the real-world requirements of that occupation.	
☐	☐	Can seek information for preferred occupation from a variety of written sources (e.g., occupational manuals, brochures, employment agency publications).	
☐	☐	Knowshow to plan and implement a specific pattern of skill preparation needed for a preferred occupation.	
☐	☐	Knows the special preparation needed for entrance into a preferred occupation.	
☐	☐	Can develop a portfolio of information and/or work samples to demonstrate knowledge of a preferred occupation.	
☐	☐	Can make the connection between (a) one's interests, strengths, and limitations, and (b) the requirements and demands of a preferred occupation.	
☐	☐	Knows how to develop a plan of how to address the gap between (a) one's existing knowledge, skills, abilities, and/or strengths, and (b) those required by a preferred occupation.	
☐	☐	Is knowledgeable of what constitutes one's need for "reasonable accommodations" on the job site of a preferred occupation.	
☐	☐	Can get to and from a job in a timely manner.	
☐	☐	Can identify the transferable skills necessary to succeed in a preferred occupation (e.g., meeting deadlines, organizing data, communication).	
☐	☐	Can ask relevant questions of a prospective employer to get information about job requirements and demands.	

Goals/ Objectives Needed	Further Assessment Needed	Transition Knowledge and Skill Statements	Notes
☐	☐	Knows competitive employment standards for preferred occupation (e.g., work rate, quality standards, attendance and punctuality, grooming).	
☐	☐	Other _____	
		2. Makes informed choices among occupational alternatives, based on his or her own interests, preferences, and abilities.	
☐	☐	Is knowledgeable of own occupational interests, aptitudes, and preferences.	
☐	☐	Can identify an array of desirable postsecondary educational/training options.	
☐	☐	Can identify the most desirable postsecondary educational or employment training option from an array of choices.	
☐	☐	Can identify sources of information regarding jobs, training, and/or education.	
☐	☐	Can seek out and evaluate trends and projections in the job market.	
☐	☐	Can cite benefits and limitations of various occupational alternatives.	
☐	☐	Can evaluate how own strengths and limitations impact on occupational alternatives.	
☐	☐	Can identify specific jobs within various job clusters appropriate to interests, preferences, and abilities.	
☐	☐	Can identify various occupational options within the community, region, and/or state.	
☐	☐	Can prepare a personal inventory of strategies to assist in making informed choices.	
☐	☐	Can plan and participate in career exploration activities (e.g., field trips, job shadowing, on-the-job training) to determine aptitudes, interests, and preferences.	
☐	☐	Makes occupational choices that are reasonable to others or justifiable for exploration.	
☐	☐	Other _____	
		3. Knows how to get a job.	
☐	☐	Knows the process of securing a job or changing jobs.	
☐	☐	Knows how to conduct a job search.	
☐	☐	Knows how to develop a resume.	

Goals/ Objectives Needed	Further Assessment Needed	Transition Knowledge and Skill Statements	Notes
☐	☐	Knows how to complete a job application.	_____
☐	☐	Knows how to complete the elements of a successful job interview.	_____
☐	☐	Knows how to practice good grooming and hygiene for contacts in the job search.	_____
☐	☐	Knows basic requirements of selected job(s) (e.g., skills, hours, dress requirements, transportation).	_____
☐	☐	Can understand relationship between work-related experiences, volunteering, and future employability.	_____
☐	☐	Knows how to advocate for self and any required reasonable job modification.	_____
☐	☐	Can participate with others (professionals, mentors, family) to develop a list of accommodations for various occupational alternatives.	_____
☐	☐	Knows how to review job sources (e.g., classified advertisements, job postings) systematically for openings.	_____
☐	☐	Knows how to develop strategies on how to address existence of disability with a potential employer (e.g., whether or not to disclose disability during interview).	_____
☐	☐	Knows how to articulate what constitutes "promotability" in general and on a particular job site.	_____
☐	☐	Knows how to access various job assistance resources (e.g., school personnel, state agencies, private agencies) and knows the strengths and limitations of each.	_____
☐	☐	Knows how to develop a personal data sheet to assist in completing application process.	_____
☐	☐	Other _____	_____

4. Demonstrates general job skills and work attitudes preferred by employers for keeping a job and advancing; may include supported employment.

Goals/ Objectives Needed	Further Assessment Needed	Transition Knowledge and Skill Statements	Notes
☐	☐	Can use abstract thinking and/or reasoning for work tasks.	_____
☐	☐	Can perform manual skills for work tasks.	_____
☐	☐	Can retain information related to job tasks.	_____
☐	☐	Can acquire new information and skills while on the job or in preparation for a job.	_____
☐	☐	Can read, interpret, and respond to written instructions for a work task.	_____
☐	☐	Can follow oral instructions for a work task.	_____

Goals/ Objectives Needed	Further Assessment Needed	Transition Knowledge and Skill Statements	Notes
☐	☐	Can perform simple math functions (addition and subtraction).	_____
☐	☐	Can take initiative to solve problems that arise while on the job.	_____
☐	☐	Knows and is able to practice behaviors inherent in keeping a job.	_____
☐	☐	Knows and understands behaviors inherent in losing a job.	_____
☐	☐	Knows concepts and behaviors inherent in career advancement.	_____
☐	☐	Can comprehend social aspects of employment.	_____
☐	☐	Can comprehend financial aspects of employment (e.g., minimum wage, salary, benefits).	_____
☐	☐	Knows how to evaluate self and work situations.	_____
☐	☐	Can make decisions related to work tasks independently.	_____
☐	☐	Can complete tasks unsupervised.	_____
☐	☐	Knows importance of supervision.	_____
☐	☐	Can respond appropriately to supervision.	_____
☐	☐	Can understand and comply with health and safety regulations and policies.	_____
☐	☐	Can work cooperatively with others.	_____
☐	☐	Can work collaboratively with others.	_____
☐	☐	Demonstrates honesty and dependability on the job.	_____
☐	☐	Can maintain a satisfactory work rate over an extended period of time (up to 8 hours).	_____
☐	☐	Can be punctual when approaching a work-related task (e.g., job interview, task, evaluation activity).	_____
☐	☐	Knows the importance of showing up for work every day or with very few absences.	_____
☐	☐	Can prepare and clean up work area when beginning and ending a day's work or a project.	_____
☐	☐	Can discriminate basic object characteristics (e.g., color, texture, shape).	_____
☐	☐	Can refrain from engaging in nonfunctional behaviors (e.g., self-mutilation, bizarre speech, public masturbation, compulsive rituals).	_____
☐	☐	Other _____	_____

Goals/ Objectives Needed	Further Assessment Needed	Transition Knowledge and Skill Statements	Notes
		5. Has the specific knowledge and skills needed to perform a particular skilled, semiskilled, or entry-level job; may include supported employment.	
☐	☐	Knows how to fix or repair tools, machinery, and/or other equipment.	
☐	☐	Knows how to handle materials and/or equipment with precision and speed.	
☐	☐	Knows how to use and maintain tools, equipment, and materials used to complete tasks.	
☐	☐	Has skills in graphic arts (e.g., drawing, graphics design, layout).	
☐	☐	Has skills in computer operations (e.g., word processing, databases, graphics, data analyses).	
☐	☐	Has skills in clerical support occupations (e.g., filing, word processing, data processing).	
☐	☐	Has skills in building trades (e.g., carpentry, masonry, plumbing).	
☐	☐	Has skills in vocational agriculture and agribusiness.	
☐	☐	Has skills in marketing and distributive occupations.	
☐	☐	Has skills in food preparation and presentation.	
☐	☐	Has skills in electronic occupations.	
☐	☐	Has skills in health care occupations or professions.	
☐	☐	Has skills in child care occupations.	
☐	☐	Has skills in creative or performance artistic skills (e.g., literature, music, art, dance).	
☐	☐	Has skills in beauty (personal services) professions.	
☐	☐	Other _____	

FURTHER EDUCATION/TRAINING

Goals/ Objectives Needed	Further Assessment Needed	Transition Knowledge and Skill Statements	Notes
		6. Knows how to gain entry into an appropriate post-school community employment training program.	
☐	☐	Can identify a list of desirable outcomes from completing a community employment training program	
☐	☐	Knows how to develop a realistic plan for accessing postsecondary education or training options.	
☐	☐	Can identify available school or community training programs.	

Goals/ Objectives Needed	Further Assessment Needed	Transition Knowledge and Skill Statements	Notes
☐	☐	Can select the postsecondary community training program that best meets student's needs.	
☐	☐	Can develop a portfolio with information necessary for entrance to an employment training program.	
☐	☐	Knows how to identify and meet any prerequisite to entrance into a postsecondary community training program.	
☐	☐	Knows how to access financial support for postsecondary community education or training programs.	
☐	☐	Knowledgeable of any prerequisite tests that are administered (e.g., procedures, requirements, time limitations, adaptations).	
☐	☐	Knowledgeable of how to evaluate services of a training program that provides support for individuals with disabilities.	
		7. Knows how to gain entry into a General Education Development (GED) program.	
☐	☐	Can identify a series of desirable outcomes from completing a GED program.	
☐	☐	Can select an appropriate GED program.	
☐	☐	Can develop a portfolio with information necessary for entrance into a GED program.	
☐	☐	Can identify and meet any prerequisite for entrance into a GED program.	
☐	☐	Knows how to access financial support for a GED program.	
☐	☐	Knows how to develop a realistic plan for accessing a GED program.	
☐	☐	Knowledgeable of any prerequisite tests that are required (e.g., procedures, time limitations, adaptations).	
		8. Knows how to gain entry into an appropriate vocational/technical school.	
☐	☐	Can identify a series of desirable outcomes from completing a vocational/technical school or program.	
☐	☐	Can select the vocational/technical school that best meets student's needs.	
☐	☐	Can develop a portfolio with information necessary for entrance into a vocational/technical school.	

Goals/ Objectives Needed	Further Assessment Needed	Transition Knowledge and Skill Statements	Notes
☐	☐	Knows how to identify and meet any prerequisite for entrance into a vocational/technical school.	
☐	☐	Knows how to access financial support for a vocational/technical school.	
☐	☐	Knows how to develop a realistic plan for accessing a vocational/technical school.	
☐	☐	Knowledgeable of how any prerequisite tests are administered (e.g., procedures, requirements, time limitations, adaptations).	
☐	☐	Knows how to evaluate the capacity of a vocational/ technical school to provide support for individuals with disabilities.	
		9. Knows how to gain entry into an appropriate college or university.	
☐	☐	Can identify a series of desirable outcomes from completing an appropriate college or university.	
☐	☐	Knows how to develop a realistic plan for accessing an appropriate college or university.	
☐	☐	Can select a college or university that best meets student's needs.	
☐	☐	Knows how to develop a portfolio with information necessary for entrance into an appropriate college or university.	
☐	☐	Knows how to identify and meet any prerequisites to entrance into an appropriate college or university.	
☐	☐	Knows how to access financial support appropriate for a college or university.	
☐	☐	Knowledgeable of any prerequisite tests that are administered (e.g., procedures, requirements, time limitations, adaptations).	
☐	☐	Knows how to apply for required entrance examinations.	
☐	☐	Knows how to participate in entrance exam preparation program (e.g., class, books, video, computer-assisted instruction).	
☐	☐	Knows how to locate a college or university and evaluate it in terms of location, costs, and programs	
☐	☐	Knows how to evaluate capacity of a college or university to provide support for individuals with disabilities.	

Goals/ Objectives Needed	Further Assessment Needed	Transition Knowledge and Skill Statements	Notes
		10. Can succeed in an appropriate postsecondary program.	
☐	☐	Can use the academic support skills (e.g., organizational skills, time management, and other study skills) necessary to succeed in a given postsecondary setting.	
☐	☐	Can perform reading skills required in the program.	
☐	☐	Can perform writing skills required in the program.	
☐	☐	Can perform math skills required in the program.	
☐	☐	Can analyze information and draw conclusions.	
☐	☐	Can manage finances.	
☐	☐	Knows how to balance priorities between classes, work, home duties, and leisure time.	
☐	☐	Knows how to use disability support services.	
☐	☐	Knows how to develop a social support system.	
☐	☐	Knows how to assess (with others) what types of support/modifications are needed.	
☐	☐	Knows how to appropriately meet with instructor (or professor) to discuss and advocate for reasonable accommodations (e.g., manner of presentation, timeliness, knowledge of necessary reasonable accommodations).	
☐	☐	Knows how to develop and implement a plan and a time line for completion of postsecondary training program.	

DAILY LIVING

Goals/ Objectives Needed	Further Assessment Needed	Transition Knowledge and Skill Statements	Notes
		11. Maintains personal grooming and hygiene.	
☐	☐	Knows how to include personal grooming and hygiene costs in monthly budget.	
☐	☐	Can perform gender-specific personal hygiene functions (e.g., shaving, menstruation care, breast and testicle examinations).	
☐	☐	Can perform personal hygiene functions that are not gender specific (e.g., bathing, grooming)	
☐	☐	Can dress appropriately for a specific situation, occasion, or weather.	
☐	☐	Can access assistance, if necessary, when purchasing clothing.	
☐	☐	Can maintain clothing (e.g., washing, ironing, and dry cleaning) when necessary.	
☐	☐	Knows how to purchase and care for clothing.	

Goals/ Objectives Needed	Further Assessment Needed	Transition Knowledge and Skill Statements	Notes
☐	☐	Can use clothing accessories (e.g., ties, jewelry) that enhance wardrobe and are appropriate to setting.	
☐	☐	Can select, purchase, and maintain footwear appropriate to setting or activity.	
☐	☐	Can organize and store clothing items.	
☐	☐	Knows how to hire, supervise, and dismiss a personal attendant, if needed.	
		12. Knows how to locate a place to live in the community; may include using agencies that provide supported living options.	
☐	☐	Knows how to evaluate and select living arrangements (e.g., independent, with or without roommate, supported, number and type of house partners).	
☐	☐	Knows how to identify strengths and limitations of various supported and independent living options.	
☐	☐	Is knowledgeable of house and/or apartment locating services and their costs, if any.	
☐	☐	Can use newspaper ads to locate an appropriate living arrangement.	
☐	☐	Is knowledgeable of and able to work with publicly funded house and apartment locating services and their eligibility requirements.	
☐	☐	Knows how to select and analyze location in relation to transportation needs for work, school, and social life.	
☐	☐	Knows how to evaluate the next most logical living arrangement for necessary modifications.	
☐	☐	Knows how to develop a list (or use a prepared one) of pertinent questions to ask a landlord or property manager.	
☐	☐	Can evaluate the cost associated with various living arrangement options.	
☐	☐	Knows how to participate in planning for the next most logical and affordable living arrangement.	
☐	☐	Knows how to complete application materials for housing.	
☐	☐	Knows how to develop a portfolio of information necessary in determining the next most logical housing arrangement and/or completing applicant materials.	
☐	☐	Knows how to understand the concept, rights, and obligations of a lease and/or other rental agreement.	

Goals/ Objectives Needed	Further Assessment Needed	Transition Knowledge and Skill Statements	Notes
☐	☐	Knows how to evaluate location for cost, safety, and convenience.	
☐	☐	Knows how to terminate living contracts with a residence in a timely manner (e.g., giving 30-day notice, terminating and/or changing utility services).	
		13. Knows how to set up an apartment, house, or other setting.	
☐	☐	Knows how to evaluate operating costs of setting up an apartment and/or house in relation to budget.	
☐	☐	Knows how to evaluate setting up a residence in terms of special needs and maintenance.	
☐	☐	Knows how to organize and store items.	
☐	☐	Knows how to evaluate and select from various options the method(s) of transporting personal belongings to a new residence (e.g., with friends and/or family, renting equipment, hiring a moving service).	
☐	☐	Knowledgeable of and/or able to establish utility services to a new residence.	
☐	☐	Knows how to pack and unpack personal belongings in such a manner as to minimize damage.	
☐	☐	Knows how to determine which utilities are necessary and affordable and which are not in a new residence (e.g., telephone, long distance service, cable).	
☐	☐	Knows how to establish utilities and other residential services.	
☐	☐	Knows how to arrange furniture and/or personal belongings in an attractive and functional manner.	
☐	☐	Knows how to plan and implement home security and safety provisions.	
		14. Performs everyday household tasks.	
☐	☐	Can follow daily, weekly, monthly, seasonal, and/or annual cleaning and maintenance schedule.	
☐	☐	Knows how to do laundry.	
☐	☐	Can use and maintain basic household appliances (e.g., stove, oven, mixer, iron, toaster, blender, can opener).	
☐	☐	Can use basic household tools (e.g., pliers, screwdriver, wrench, hammer, saw).	
☐	☐	Knowledgeable of function and basic maintenance for household items (e.g., heater, air conditioner, washer and dryer).	

Goals/ Objectives Needed	Further Assessment Needed	Transition Knowledge and Skill Statements	Notes
☐	☐	Knows how to shop for food and other household items and stay within budget.	_____
☐	☐	Can read and complete a recipe or otherwise prepare meals.	_____ _____
☐	☐	Can read instructions and complete a prepared and/or box mix.	_____ _____
☐	☐	Knows how to store food properly.	_____
☐	☐	Knows how to perform home maintenance (e.g., sweeping, mopping, vacuuming).	_____ _____
☐	☐	Knows how to wash and store dishes and other cooking and eating equipment.	_____ _____
☐	☐	Knows how to operate and clean basic appliances (e.g., toaster, blender, stove, iron).	_____ _____
☐	☐	Knows how to pick up items around residence and return to proper setting.	_____ _____
☐	☐	Knows how to make bed, change sheets, wash sheets and blankets, and adjust bed linen seasonally.	_____ _____
☐	☐	Can supervise personal attendant who performs daily living services.	_____ _____

15. Manages own money.

Goals/ Objectives Needed	Further Assessment Needed	Transition Knowledge and Skill Statements	Notes
☐	☐	Can manipulate money (e.g., selecting coins and/or bills to total a specific amount, make change).	_____ _____
☐	☐	Can identify coins and bills and their value.	_____
☐	☐	Can pay bills in a timely fashion.	_____
☐	☐	Knows how to apply for a loan and how loans are processed.	_____ _____
☐	☐	Knows what type of documentation is included in a credit history.	_____ _____
☐	☐	Knowledgeable of the short- and long-term impact of a good or bad credit history.	_____ _____
☐	☐	Knowledgeable of impact of interest rates on payments and personal finance.	_____ _____
☐	☐	Knows how to open and use checking account.	_____
☐	☐	Knows how to open and use savings account.	_____
☐	☐	Knows how to evaluate costs and services and then select a bank, credit union, and/or savings and loan corporation for personal financial services.	_____ _____ _____
☐	☐	Can plan and use simple weekly, monthly, and annual budgets.	_____ _____

Goals/ Objectives Needed	Further Assessment Needed	Transition Knowledge and Skill Statements	Notes
☐	☐	Knows how credit cards function and how to select payment schedules.	
☐	☐	Knows how to purchase large items that may require financing.	
☐	☐	Can participate with others in developing a long- and short-term financial plan.	
☐	☐	Can participate in cost-saving techniques (comparative shopping, coupon use, sales, discount thrift, bulk buying).	
☐	☐	Knows how to evaluate need for and purchase necessary insurance policies.	
☐	☐	Can use an automatic teller machine and/or debit card.	
☐	☐	Can use an automatic teller machine and/or debit card responsibly.	
☐	☐	Can use a telephone and/or computer banking system.	
☐	☐	Can use a telephone and/or computer banking system responsibly.	
☐	☐	Can evaluate payment options (e.g., cash, credit, lay-away) on a purchase and the benefits and limitations of each.	
☐	☐	Knows differences in various types of interest options (e.g., simple, compound, and revolving interests) and their impact.	

16. Uses local transportation systems when needed.

Goals/ Objectives Needed	Further Assessment Needed	Transition Knowledge and Skill Statements	Notes
☐	☐	Knows local transportation options.	
☐	☐	Can use public transportation.	
☐	☐	Knowledgeable of the process involved in getting a standard driver's license.	
☐	☐	Knowledgeable of the process involved in getting a special or restricted driver's license (due to special needs such as bioptics, or modified car or van).	
☐	☐	Knows how to use a safety belt in a vehicle and/or a helmet with a bicycle or motorcycle.	
☐	☐	Knowledgeable of the hazards associated with driving under the influence of alcohol.	
☐	☐	Knowledgeable of the impact of a driving violation record on transportation options and costs.	
☐	☐	Can incorporate transportation costs into budget.	

Goals/ Objectives Needed	Further Assessment Needed	Transition Knowledge and Skill Statements	Notes
☐	☐	Can estimate time needed for transportation (especially public) and incorporate into planning.	
☐	☐	Can demonstrate appropriate social behaviors on public transportation.	
☐	☐	Can travel independently to and from inter- or intracity destination.	
☐	☐	Can plan routes to and from various destinations.	
☐	☐	Can participate in independent travel to increasingly more distant destinations (e.g., classroom, neighborhood, city).	
☐	☐	Can identify need for, evaluate options for, budget for, and purchase auto insurance.	
☐	☐	Knows how to access special transportation services available for persons with disabilities.	
☐	☐	Can solve transportation crises (e.g., car being repaired, need for temporary transportation).	

LEISURE ACTIVITIES

17. Performs various indoor leisure activities.

Goals/ Objectives Needed	Further Assessment Needed	Transition Knowledge and Skill Statements	Notes
☐	☐	Can initiate and/or participate in structured solo indoor activities.	
☐	☐	Can initiate and/or participate in unstructured solo indoor activities.	
☐	☐	Can initiate and/or participate in structured team and/or group indoor activities.	
☐	☐	Can initiate and/or participate in unstructured team and/or group indoor activities.	
☐	☐	Can cooperate with others in indoor leisure activities.	
☐	☐	Can participate in five to eight preferred participatory indoor activities.	
☐	☐	Can participate in five to eight preferred spectator indoor activities.	
☐	☐	Can develop, maintain, and improve specific skills that increase performance on selected activities (practice).	
☐	☐	Can and is willing to try new indoor leisure activities.	
☐	☐	Can manage time to allow for indoor leisure options.	
☐	☐	Can participate in physical (individual and group) indoor activities (e.g., aerobics, weight training, bowling).	

Goals/ Objectives Needed	Further Assessment Needed	Transition Knowledge and Skill Statements	Notes
☐	☐	Can budget for equipment, fees, and other costs associated with desired activities.	
☐	☐	Can participate in table or electronic games.	
☐	☐	Can participate in art, hobby, and/or craft activities.	
☐	☐	Can follow through with commitments to self and others to participate in activities.	
☐	☐	Can practice good sportsmanship.	

18. Performs various outdoor leisure activities.

Goals/ Objectives Needed	Further Assessment Needed	Transition Knowledge and Skill Statements	Notes
☐	☐	Can initiate and/or participate in structured solo outdoor activities.	
☐	☐	Can initiate and/or participate in unstructured solo outdoor activities.	
☐	☐	Can initiate and/or participate in structured group outdoor activities.	
☐	☐	Can initiate and/or participate in unstructured team and/or group outdoor activities.	
☐	☐	Can cooperate with others in outdoor leisure activities.	
☐	☐	Can participate in five to eight preferred participatory outdoor activities.	
☐	☐	Can participate in five to eight preferred spectator outdoor activities.	
☐	☐	Can follow through with commitments to self and others to participate in outdoor activities.	
☐	☐	Can budget for equipment, fees, and other costs associated with desired activities.	
☐	☐	Can develop, maintain, and improve specific skills that increase performance on selected activities.	
☐	☐	Can and is willing to try new outdoor leisure activities.	
☐	☐	Can manage time to allow for outdoor leisure options.	
☐	☐	Can practice safety and not take unnecessary risks in performing outdoor activities.	
☐	☐	Can practice good sportsmanship.	

19. Uses settings that provide various types of entertainment.

Goals/ Objectives Needed	Further Assessment Needed	Transition Knowledge and Skill Statements	Notes
☐	☐	Can access local entertainment options (e.g., movies, plays, sports, parks).	

Goals/ Objectives Needed	Further Assessment Needed	Transition Knowledge and Skill Statements	Notes
☐	☐	Can make reservations for special events and at restaurants when needed.	
☐	☐	Can budget for entertainment activities.	
☐	☐	Knows how to evaluate capacity or capability of a facility to meet special needs (e.g., mobility, auditory, and descriptive services).	
☐	☐	Can access transportation in a timely and cost-effective manner in order to access a wide variety of entertainment options.	
☐	☐	Can initiate and participate with others in a variety of entertainment options.	
☐	☐	Can participate in socially oriented situations (e.g., dinners at restaurants, parties, concerts, nightclubs).	
☐	☐	Can participate in neighborhood activities (e.g., garage sales, block parties, barbecues).	
☐	☐	Can participate in special events (e.g., county fairs; trade, hobby, home and/or garden shows; parades; festivals).	
☐	☐	Can identify and participate in free entertainment options.	
☐	☐	Can develop short- and long-term (more than 30 days) plans for participation in various types of entertainment.	
☐	☐	Can interact appropriately during activities (e.g., limiting talking, waiting in line, purchasing passes).	

COMMUNITY PARTICIPATION

20. Knows his or her basic legal rights.

Goals/ Objectives Needed	Further Assessment Needed	Transition Knowledge and Skill Statements	Notes
☐	☐	Knowledgeable of legal aspects of employment (e.g., minimum wage, withholding, worker's compensation).	
☐	☐	Knows personal and employment rights under the Americans with Disabilities Act, Section 504 of the Rehabilitation Act of 1973, and the Social Security Act.	
☐	☐	Knows what typically constitutes "reasonable accommodations" in school, work, and postsecondary training.	
☐	☐	Knowledgeable of sexual harassment and legal options when it occurs.	
☐	☐	Knows basic rights afforded to all citizens.	
☐	☐	Knows rights for self-determination after 18 years of age.	

Goals/ Objectives Needed	Further Assessment Needed	Transition Knowledge and Skill Statements	Notes
☐	☐	Knows of obligation to register for the military draft, if male.	
☐	☐	Knows what type of information is appropriate and not appropriate to give employers.	
☐	☐	Knowledgeable of how legal rights interact with daily living routines.	
☐	☐	Knows what constitutes a legal contract.	
☐	☐	Knowledgeable of common legal commitments (e.g., marriage, loans, employment contracts).	

21. Participates as an active citizen.

Goals/ Objectives Needed	Further Assessment Needed	Transition Knowledge and Skill Statements	Notes
☐	☐	Can adhere to the attributes of a good citizen (e.g., obeying laws, respecting environment).	
☐	☐	Knows voter registration process and requirements.	
☐	☐	Knows voting process and voting locations (if applicable).	
☐	☐	Knows tax concepts and his or her responsibility for paying taxes.	
☐	☐	Can use personal and/or public property responsibly.	
☐	☐	Knows how to obtain a copy of his or her birth certificate.	
☐	☐	Knows how to report a suspected crime to authorities.	
☐	☐	Knowledgeable of responsibility for and ability to participate in jury service.	
☐	☐	Can volunteer to assist an organization, club, social action group, or other community service organization.	
☐	☐	Can practice respect for others' privacy and act to protect his or her own.	

22. Makes legal decisions affecting his or her life.

Goals/ Objectives Needed	Further Assessment Needed	Transition Knowledge and Skill Statements	Notes
☐	☐	Can learn about changes in laws in the community, state, and nation.	
☐	☐	Can understand basic principles, rights, and responsibilities of entering into a contract (written and verbal).	
☐	☐	Can understand long- and short-term consequences of choosing whether or not to break a law.	
☐	☐	Can understand difference between civil and criminal legal issues.	

Goals/ Objectives Needed	Further Assessment Needed	Transition Knowledge and Skill Statements	Notes
☐	☐	Can understand impact of and differences in felony and misdemeanor offenses.	
☐	☐	Knows how to use laws designed to impact and protect individuals with disabilities for personal situations.	
☐	☐	Knows how to access legal assistance.	
☐	☐	Can understand that individuals are obligated to follow laws and the various penalties for not doing so (e.g., ticket, probation, fine, incarceration).	
☐	☐	Can understand and advocate for his or her right to privacy.	
☐	☐	Can determine if legal rights, property, or person are violated and how to file charges and/or lawsuit.	
☐	☐	Knowledgeable of "Miranda" rights (e.g., right to an attorney).	
☐	☐	Can understand the importance of signing any legal document or agreement.	
☐	☐	Can seek assistance if he or she needs additional information about a legal issue (e.g., from a parent, relative, mentor, lawyer, or legal adviser).	

23. Locates appropriate community services and resources.

Goals/ Objectives Needed	Further Assessment Needed	Transition Knowledge and Skill Statements	Notes
☐	☐	Can evaluate various community services for effectiveness and efficiency in meeting his or her needs (e.g., transportation, costs, service options).	
☐	☐	Can identify, locate, and access personal services (e.g., hair maintenance, grocery stores, repair services).	
☐	☐	Can identify any clubs or organizations that persons might want to join (e.g., hiking club, church groups or activities, movie or book clubs).	
☐	☐	Can locate post office.	
☐	☐	Can locate community mental health services.	
☐	☐	Can locate community recreational services.	
☐	☐	Can locate community medical services.	
☐	☐	Can locate community advocacy services.	
☐	☐	Can locate community legal services.	
☐	☐	Can locate community emergency assistance.	
☐	☐	Can locate community religious groups for religious participation or use of available services.	

Goals/ Objectives Needed	Further Assessment Needed	Transition Knowledge and Skill Statements	Notes
☐	☐	Can locate public pay telephones, vending machines, and restrooms.	_____
☐	☐	Can locate information in the phone book (e.g., white, yellow, index, and community resource pages).	_____
		24. Knows how to use a variety of services and resources successfully.	_____
☐	☐	Can operate a vending machine.	_____
☐	☐	Can use local area retail businesses and services (e.g., restaurants, department stores, shoe stores, cleaners).	_____
☐	☐	Can use public services (e.g., bank, post office) in local area.	_____
☐	☐	Can select and attend movies, plays, sporting events, or other structured attractions.	_____
☐	☐	Can use a telephone directory (e.g., white and yellow pages).	_____
☐	☐	Can use public pay and private telephones.	_____
☐	☐	Can demonstrate appropriate interpersonal skills in order to obtain services or access to resources.	_____
☐	☐	Can access entitlement and eligibility service systems.	_____
☐	☐	Can access attendant care resources.	_____
☐	☐	Can solicit, accept, and refuse assistance with dignity.	_____
☐	☐	Can follow through with a service provider.	_____
☐	☐	Can develop a network of service providers and/or circle of friends to meet personal needs.	_____
		25. Knows how to obtain financial assistance from specific state and federal agencies.	_____
☐	☐	Knows basic roles and functions of relevant major state and federal agencies.	_____
☐	☐	Can identify roles, responsibilities, and benefits potentially available from specific state and federal agencies.	_____
☐	☐	Knows eligibility requirements for major state and federal agencies.	_____
☐	☐	Can follow through with assistance provider in order to achieve and retain financial assistance.	_____
☐	☐	Can register for and access Medicaid.	_____
☐	☐	Can register for and access entitlement programs of the Social Security Administration.	_____

Goals/ Objectives Needed	Further Assessment Needed	Transition Knowledge and Skill Statements	Notes
☐	☐	Can register for and access food stamps and other social service assistance.	
☐	☐	Can register for and access student loan services.	
☐	☐	Can identify potential discrimination by financial institutions who are under state and/or federal requirements not to discriminate.	
☐	☐	Knows how to develop a portfolio with information required in order to access financial assistance.	
☐	☐	Knows how to evaluate effectiveness of financial assistance.	
☐	☐	Knows how to advocate for modification of services and/or increasing, decreasing, or modifying existing services.	

HEALTH

26. Maintains good physical health.

Goals/ Objectives Needed	Further Assessment Needed	Transition Knowledge and Skill Statements	Notes
☐	☐	Can participate in age-appropriate fine and gross motor activities.	
☐	☐	Knows own physical self.	
☐	☐	Knowledgeable of the nature of his or her disability.	
☐	☐	Can practice exercises to maintain typical range of motion.	
☐	☐	Can perform physical tasks with typical levels of strength, stamina, and flexibility.	
☐	☐	Can differentiate between over-the-counter and prescription medication.	
☐	☐	Can practice good posture.	
☐	☐	Knows how to monitor weight.	
☐	☐	Able to develop and implement a plan to change weight, if necessary.	
☐	☐	Can exercise regularly.	
☐	☐	Knowledgeable of his or her physical needs.	
☐	☐	Knowledgeable of medical history and how to obtain relevant records.	
☐	☐	Can practice healthy sleeping behaviors.	
☐	☐	Knows how to practice preventative health care.	
☐	☐	Able to plan menus for various periods of time (day, week, month) to follow a prescribed diet.	

Goals/ Objectives Needed	Further Assessment Needed	Transition Knowledge and Skill Statements	Notes
☐	☐	Knowledgeable of interplay between nutrition, taste, and budget.	
☐	☐	Can practice eating behaviors that are appropriate to the setting and occasion.	
☐	☐	Knowledgeable of food groups and minimum daily requirements.	
☐	☐	Knowledgeable of relationship between food intake, exercise, and weight maintenance.	
☐	☐	Knows how to access special equipment (assistive devices) necessary to increase independent eating.	
☐	☐	Can store food appropriately and safely.	
☐	☐	Knows and can perform basic sanitation practices for handling food.	
☐	☐	Knows general safety practices at home and in the community.	
☐	☐	Can interpret physical symptoms of pain and discomfort and knows how to find out what is wrong.	
☐	☐	Knows effects of use and misuse of alcohol, tobacco, and drugs.	

27. Addresses physical problems that arise.

☐	☐	Can locate and use a pharmacy to fill prescription.	
☐	☐	Can identify common and basic illness prevention techniques.	
☐	☐	Can identify common basic treatment techniques for physical problems that do not require a doctor or prescription.	
☐	☐	Can use basic first aid procedures.	
☐	☐	Knows what to do if quick (but not emergency) medical attention is needed.	
☐	☐	Can get information on side effects of prescriptions from a pharmacist.	
☐	☐	Knowledgeable of identification, prevention, and treatment for sexually transmitted diseases.	
☐	☐	Knows how to find a new doctor.	
☐	☐	Knows how to use and maintain orthotics, prosthetics, or other disability-specific devices or health needs.	
☐	☐	Can take necessary medications independently, according to instructions.	

Goals/ Objectives Needed	Further Assessment Needed	Transition Knowledge and Skill Statements	Notes
☐	☐	Knows how and when to seek a doctor for preventative medicine or treatment.	
☐	☐	Demonstrates ability to enroll and participate in a health insurance plan.	
		28. Maintains good mental health.	
☐	☐	Can identify sources of stress and the effects on mental or physical health.	
☐	☐	Can practice stress-reduction and stress-management techniques.	
☐	☐	Can identify one's basic psychological needs (e.g., acceptance, recognition, nurturing).	
☐	☐	Can maintain consistent moods and behavior patterns.	
☐	☐	Can identify fears, anger, and depression and respond appropriately.	
☐	☐	Knows how to seek and participate in genetic counseling, if warranted.	
☐	☐	Can understand psychological impact that a disability may have on an individual.	
☐	☐	Can cope with changes in interpersonal relationships.	
☐	☐	Can identify and describe events that may trigger adverse change in behavior.	
☐	☐	Can make choices that reflect his or her values, and then follow through with appropriate actions.	
☐	☐	Can recognize personal responsibility in controlling his or her behavior.	
☐	☐	Can realistically assess how susceptible he or she is to excessive and/or abusive behavior.	
☐	☐	Can take prescribed medication appropriately.	
		29. Addresses mental health problems that arise.	
☐	☐	Can obtain emotional support for disability-related mental health needs.	
☐	☐	Can identify excessive and/or abusive behaviors.	
☐	☐	Can understand how excessive and/or abusive behaviors affect victims (including self).	
☐	☐	Can develop a relationship with someone (e.g., friend, professional, mentor) with whom he or she can confide.	

Goals/ Objectives Needed	Further Assessment Needed	Transition Knowledge and Skill Statements	Notes
☐	☐	Can verbalize emotional needs.	_____
☐	☐	Can identify self-defeating behaviors.	_____
☐	☐	Can develop and implement a plan (with others) to minimize and eliminate self-defeating behaviors.	_____
☐	☐	Can practice strategies to minimize effects of stress.	_____
☐	☐	Can identify and implement strategies to improve self-esteem.	_____
☐	☐	Can enter into a trusting relationship.	_____
☐	☐	Can take medication as prescribed.	_____
☐	☐	Can recognize warning signs of addiction, depression, and/or other possible mental health inhibitors.	_____
☐	☐	Can use strategies for refusing illicit substances.	_____
		30. Knows how reproductive system works.	_____
☐	☐	Knowledgeable of primary sexual characteristics of males and females.	_____
☐	☐	Knowledgeable of conception process.	_____
☐	☐	Knowledgeable of pregnancy process.	_____
☐	☐	Knowledgeable of birth process.	_____
☐	☐	Knowledgeable of characteristics of sexually transmitted diseases.	_____
☐	☐	Knowledgeable of cause and impact of sexually transmitted diseases.	_____
☐	☐	Knowledgeable of human sexual response characteristics.	_____
☐	☐	Knowledgeable of methods of birth control, including abstinence.	_____
☐	☐	Knowledgeable of role, function, and impact of hormones, especially as they relate to reproduction.	_____
☐	☐	Knowledgeable of and knows how to minimize and treat menstrual discomfort, if female.	_____
☐	☐	Knowledgeable of role of masturbation in human sexuality.	_____
☐	☐	Knowledgeable of physical and emotional changes associated with adolescence and their relationship to the reproductive system.	_____

Goals/ Objectives Needed	Further Assessment Needed	Transition Knowledge and Skill Statements	Notes
		31. Makes informed choices regarding sexual behavior.	
☐	☐	Can express sexuality in socially, emotionally, and age-appropriate behavior.	
☐	☐	Knowledgeable of and able to differentiate public from private behaviors (e.g., types of touching, hugging, kissing).	
☐	☐	Knows the importance of privacy for engaging in sexual behavior.	
☐	☐	Can understand that sexual attitudes, beliefs, values, and lifestyles are unique to the individual, and the impact of that uniqueness.	
☐	☐	Knows what constitutes criminal sexual activities and the consequences (e.g., sexual misconduct, abuse, rape, date rape, harassment).	
☐	☐	Can understand the impact that sexual activity may have on his or her partner's quality of life (e.g., pregnancy, sexually transmitted diseases, financial and health implications).	
☐	☐	Can understand options should a pregnancy result, and the consequences of each option.	
☐	☐	Knows of various types of birth control methods, including abstinence, and the strengths and limitations of each.	
☐	☐	Knows how to prevent, identify, and seek treatment for sexually transmitted diseases.	
☐	☐	Knows how to ask a person for a date (e.g., group and individual dates).	
☐	☐	Can differentiate between sexuality and love and the emotional consequences of sexual activities.	
☐	☐	Can identify personal and family attitudes, values, and cultural mores as they relate to sexual decision making.	
☐	☐	Can identify gender orientation.	
☐	☐	Can identify role of sexual behavior in varying degrees of committed and noncommitted relationships.	
☐	☐	Can begin, maintain, and end intimate relationships.	
☐	☐	Can differentiate between typical sexual impulses and atypical or deviant impulses, and seek assistance in controlling and/or eliminating these impulses.	

Goals/ Objectives Needed	Further Assessment Needed	Transition Knowledge and Skill Statements	Notes
		SELF-DETERMINATION	
		32. Recognizes and accepts his or her strengths and limitations.	
☐	☐	Can identify his or her guiding values.	
☐	☐	Can prioritize values from an array.	
☐	☐	Can practice reflective thinking in evaluation of personal strengths and limitations.	
☐	☐	Can identify his or her accomplishments.	
☐	☐	Can identify his or her failures, and factors that contributed to the lack of success.	
☐	☐	Can actively participate in development of his or her Individualized Transition Plan or Individualized Education Program.	
☐	☐	Can identify other's perceptions of him- or herself.	
☐	☐	Can set well-defined and realistic personal goals.	
☐	☐	Can follow through with achievement of personal goals.	
☐	☐	Can understand and practice time/task management skills.	
☐	☐	Can use judgment when determining when to increase level of independence while performing task and/or goal.	
☐	☐	Can draw conclusions from reflective thinking and develop a plan for adjustments if necessary.	
☐	☐	Can recognize when being taken advantage of by others and take steps to stop it.	
		33. Expresses feelings and ideas to others appropriately.	
☐	☐	Can differentiate among various levels of self-disclosure that are appropriate to a setting and degree of friendship.	
☐	☐	Can identify when an event or situation is causing discomfort and to express that discomfort appropriately.	
☐	☐	Can present his or her side of a conflict.	
☐	☐	Can limit conversational subjects, ideas, and/or feelings to the appropriate setting.	
☐	☐	Can modulate volume of speech appropriate to the situation.	

Goals/ Objectives Needed	Further Assessment Needed	Transition Knowledge and Skill Statements	Notes
☐	☐	Can describe benefits of following social conventions when expressing feelings and/or ideas.	
☐	☐	Can use a variety of expressive formats for expressing feelings and/or ideas (e.g., letters, verbal and nonverbal communication, artistic expressions).	
☐	☐	Can use language (e.g., formal, slang, technical) appropriate to the situations and communication partners.	
☐	☐	Can show tact when expressing feelings and/or ideas.	
☐	☐	Can show how setting, communication partner, and desired outcome impact how and when to appropriately express feelings and/or ideas.	
☐	☐	Can respond to a situation with an appropriate level of intensity.	

34. Expresses feelings and ideas to others confidently.

Goals/ Objectives Needed	Further Assessment Needed	Transition Knowledge and Skill Statements	Notes
☐	☐	Can define and/or list a variety of feeling words (e.g., *love, hate, miss, hope, anxious, eager, dread*).	
☐	☐	Can respond with feeling words appropriate to the situation and other participants.	
☐	☐	Can maintain a relationship with a friend or confidante.	
☐	☐	Can speak positively about him- or herself.	
☐	☐	Can express own strengths and limitations to others.	
☐	☐	Can identify and express a wide variety of feelings clearly and concisely.	
☐	☐	Can identify and express a goal, hope, and/or dream.	
☐	☐	Can identify potential benefits of sharing feelings and/or ideas with another person.	
☐	☐	Can be assertive (versus passive or aggressive) when expressing desires or responding to others.	
☐	☐	Can try an alternative method to express him- or herself when not understood by another.	
☐	☐	Can identify situations in which it may be difficult to express feelings and/or ideas, and then develop a strategy to do so.	
☐	☐	Can express feelings and/or ideas about the existence of his or her disability.	
☐	☐	Can recognize impact of teasing, sarcasm, and offensive jokes on self and others.	
☐	☐	Can express feelings and ideas in a timely manner.	

Goals/ Objectives Needed	Further Assessment Needed	Transition Knowledge and Skill Statements	Notes
		35. Sets personal goals.	
☐	☐	Can identify an array of personal goals.	
☐	☐	Can prioritize and select one or two goals to work on.	
☐	☐	Can define a goal outcome in measurable or identifiable terms.	
☐	☐	Can define (behaviorally and mentally) barriers (e.g., internal, situational, and resource limitations) to completing a goal.	
☐	☐	Can define (behaviorally and mentally) benefits of completing a goal.	
☐	☐	Can describe resources and alternatives necessary to goal completion.	
☐	☐	Can develop and prioritize behavioral steps (or actions) necessary to complete a goal.	
☐	☐	Can set "subgoals" or benchmarks along path to a goal.	
☐	☐	Can make adjustments in the plan or in strategies when the path to the goal is "derailed."	
☐	☐	Can access resources if path to a goal is "derailed."	
☐	☐	Can develop a time line or target date for completion of intermediate steps or subgoals (e.g., "achieve behavior X by July 1").	
☐	☐	Can acknowledge and celebrate completion of a goal.	
		36. Makes personal decisions.	
☐	☐	Can identify guiding values underlying a personal decision.	
☐	☐	Can take personal ownership of values by consciously vocalizing, writing, or otherwise demonstrating values.	
☐	☐	Can take initiative to solve problems.	
☐	☐	Can vocalize reasons and/or rationale for a decision.	
☐	☐	Can develop a variety of options in preparation for making a decision.	
☐	☐	Can evaluate options in terms of effectiveness, cost, functionality, and social conventions.	
☐	☐	Can seek information from a variety of sources and formats (e.g., written, personal experiences of others).	
☐	☐	Can determine when it is appropriate to make a quick decision versus a reflective decision.	

Goals/ Objectives Needed	Further Assessment Needed	Transition Knowledge and Skill Statements	Notes
☐	☐	Can make informed decisions for personal grooming styles.	
☐	☐	Can make informed decisions on health-related issues (e.g., nutrition).	
☐	☐	Can make informed consumer decisions.	
☐	☐	Can make informed decisions for leisure activities.	
☐	☐	Can make informed decisions for community participation.	
☐	☐	Can make informed decisions for interpersonal relationships.	
☐	☐	Can practice a variety of strategies and activities to maximize decision making and/or problem solving.	
☐	☐	Can follow through on decisions requiring action.	
☐	☐	Can make informed decisions on programs and services needed for improving quality of life (e.g., employment, socialization, health, mental health, transportation).	

COMMUNICATION

Goals/ Objectives Needed	Further Assessment Needed	Transition Knowledge and Skill Statements	Notes
		37. Has needed speaking skills; may include sign language or alternative/augmentative communication.	
☐	☐	Can engage in conversational speech (e.g., several exchanges on single or related topics).	
☐	☐	Can initiate conversation with others.	
☐	☐	Can maintain eye contact during conversation.	
☐	☐	Can speak clearly and at an appropriate decibel level.	
☐	☐	Can end conversation appropriately.	
☐	☐	Can give simple and complex directions.	
☐	☐	Can use expressive language without drawing attention because of vocabulary, syntax, or grammar.	
☐	☐	Can differentiate between passive, aggressive, and assertive speech.	
☐	☐	Can give feedback to others that is timely, action oriented, and specific to the situation.	
☐	☐	Knows role of nonverbal communication in speaking skills.	
☐	☐	Demonstrates ability to interpret and to use nonverbal communication in speaking.	

Goals/ Objectives Needed	Further Assessment Needed	Transition Knowledge and Skill Statements	Notes
☐	☐	Can ask relevant and timely questions.	
☐	☐	Can tell jokes or anecdotes.	
☐	☐	Can modulate voice appropriate to situation, mood, purpose, and intended result of communication.	
☐	☐	Can communicate a persuasive, clear, and concise message that contains basic information.	
☐	☐	Can solicit information for a specific cause.	
		38. Has needed listening skills; may include sign language, speech reading, or other assistive technology/services.	
☐	☐	Can practice active listening skills.	
☐	☐	Can maintain appropriate eye contact while listening to others.	
☐	☐	Can comprehend simple and complex directions.	
☐	☐	Knows role of nonverbal communication in listening skills.	
☐	☐	Can differentiate among comments that are positive, negative, and neutral, and among informational comments, demands, and requests.	
☐	☐	Can limit interrupting a communication partner.	
☐	☐	Can identify and attend to an important or relevant sound or speaker from an array of environmental sounds.	
☐	☐	Can recognize key words and concluding or summarizing phrases.	
☐	☐	Can develop mental imagery from what is heard.	
☐	☐	Can identify details from what is heard.	
☐	☐	Can use contextual cues to assist in determining word meaning or other relevant information.	
☐	☐	Can identify feelings and intent of speaker based on words, tone of voice, and nonverbal communication.	
☐	☐	Can understand jokes or anecdotes.	
		39. Has needed reading skills for acquiring information from written materials; may include tactile systems or other assistive technology/services.	
☐	☐	Can seek additional training or skill development necessary to effectively and efficiently access written information (e.g., Braille, speech output devices, spellers).	
☐	☐	Can read information and identify the main idea.	

Goals/ Objectives Needed	Further Assessment Needed	Transition Knowledge and Skill Statements	Notes
☐	☐	Can read information and identify the setting.	
☐	☐	Can read information and identify the plot.	
☐	☐	Can read information and make judgments and draw conclusions about the characters.	
☐	☐	Can read and summarize information.	
☐	☐	Can read information and predict outcomes.	
☐	☐	Can read information and distinguish fact and fiction.	
☐	☐	Can use various sources of information and references (e.g., dictionary, newspaper, phone book, television listings, encyclopedia).	
☐	☐	Can practice strategies to increase comprehension skills.	
☐	☐	Can read labels and follow directions.	
☐	☐	Can read and comprehend instructions on common consumer products.	
☐	☐	Can read and comprehend a newspaper article.	
☐	☐	Can read and comprehend literary and technical information (e.g., manuals, instruction booklets).	
☐	☐	Can choose reading medium that is efficient for specific task (e.g., Braille, speech output, and print).	
		40. Has needed writing skills; may include Braille systems and alternative/augmentative communication.	
☐	☐	Can produce print for others to read (e.g., use of assistive devices).	
☐	☐	Can write short sentences or phrases.	
☐	☐	Can write short paragraphs.	
☐	☐	Can satisfactorily complete a 2- to 3-page written assignment.	
☐	☐	Can satisfactorily complete a 10- to 15-page written assignment.	
☐	☐	Can write in a variety of styles appropriate to the situation and/or purpose.	
☐	☐	Can evaluate, proofread, and modify written communication.	
☐	☐	Can advocate for and participate in training necessary for writing in an alternative form of literacy (e.g., Braille and/or an alternative assistive device).	

Goals/ Objectives Needed	Further Assessment Needed	Transition Knowledge and Skill Statements	Notes
☐	☐	Can operate a familiar software program independently (e.g., word processing, spreadsheet).	
☐	☐	Can advocate and plan for the acquisition of an alternative assistive writing device.	
☐	☐	Can take personal notes.	
☐	☐	Knows the appropriate assistive devices necessary for writing, as determined by his or her specific disability.	

INTERPERSONAL RELATIONSHIPS

41. Gets along well with family members; may include parents, siblings, or other relatives.

☐	☐	Can show loyalty to other family members.	
☐	☐	Knows how to respond appropriately to accidental or intentional physical exchanges (e.g., touching, rough-housing, poking, bumping) with other family members.	
☐	☐	Can assume responsibilities in caring for and about family members.	
☐	☐	Can communicate meaningfully with other family members.	
☐	☐	Can accept and give praise.	
☐	☐	Can accept and give criticism.	
☐	☐	Knows how one's behavior may affect family members.	
☐	☐	Knows how to handle competition with family members.	
☐	☐	Can show respect for family's cultural, ethnic, or economic status.	
☐	☐	Can identify members of extended family.	
☐	☐	Can participate in mature, age-appropriate, nurturing child–parent relationships.	
☐	☐	Can remember birthdays, anniversaries, and other family celebrations.	
☐	☐	Can maintain contact with family members via phone, mail, and/or electronic mail.	
☐	☐	Can participate in family duties, chores, and celebrations.	
☐	☐	Can respect family members' space and property.	

Goals/ Objectives Needed	Further Assessment Needed	Transition Knowledge and Skill Statements	Notes
		42. Knowledgeable of and possesses skills of parenting.	
☐	☐	Knows health care issues for an infant.	
☐	☐	Knows health care issues for a preschool child.	
☐	☐	Knows heath care issues for a primary and/or intermediate child.	
☐	☐	Knows how to seek counsel from others when assistance is needed (e.g., doctor, nurse, experienced relative).	
☐	☐	Knows the emotional development of various stages of childhood.	
☐	☐	Knows the physical development of various stages of childhood.	
☐	☐	Knows how to budget for child-rearing costs (e.g., personal and hygiene needs, day care/baby-sitting).	
☐	☐	Knows the full range of responsibilities inherent in parenthood (e.g., emotional, legal, financial).	
☐	☐	Knows the importance of practicing a consistent and multileveled discipline plan.	
☐	☐	Knows the differences inherent in and the impact of raising a child in a single-parent and/or two-parent family.	
☐	☐	Knows various types of division of labor in families.	
		43. Establishes and maintains close and/or casual friendships in a variety of settings.	
☐	☐	Can respond appropriately to accidental or intentional physical exchanges (e.g., touching, roughhousing, poking, bumping) with peers and coworkers.	
☐	☐	Can show warmth and caring to others.	
☐	☐	Can adapt to changes in groups or interpersonal relationships.	
☐	☐	Can respond appropriately to good-natured teasing.	
☐	☐	Can handle competition from peers with grace and manners.	
☐	☐	Can be loyal to peers and groups.	
☐	☐	Can show sensitivity to others' feelings.	
☐	☐	Can develop and maintain friendships with more than one significant peer.	

Goals/ Objectives Needed	Further Assessment Needed	Transition Knowledge and Skill Statements	Notes
☐	☐	Can develop and maintain a friendship with an adult.	_____
☐	☐	Can maintain a friendship over an extended period of time.	_____
☐	☐	Can interact positively with individuals who are younger.	_____
☐	☐	Knows how to join a group event or activity that is already in progress.	_____
☐	☐	Can accept responsibility for his or her behavior rather than blaming others.	_____
☐	☐	Can handle conflict in interpersonal relationships.	_____
☐	☐	Can show flexibility and adaptability in interacting with others.	_____
☐	☐	Can identify critical characteristics of how to facilitate social relationships.	_____
☐	☐	Can appropriately initiate and engage in conversation with peers of the opposite sex.	_____
☐	☐	Can appropriately initiate and engage in activities with peers of the opposite sex.	_____
☐	☐	Can identify the critical barriers to developing and maintaining social relationships at work.	_____
☐	☐	Can use active listening skills and respect confidentiality.	_____
☐	☐	Can identify how others perceive self.	_____
☐	☐	Knowledgeable of the role of first impressions in establishing a relationship.	_____
☐	☐	Can understand and accept that all relationships experience personal conflicts.	_____
		44. Knowledgeable of appropriate social behavior in a variety of settings.	_____
☐	☐	Can modify social behavior in response to the setting.	_____
☐	☐	Knows about basic risks in interacting with strangers and other individuals exhibiting certain inappropriate behaviors.	_____
☐	☐	Can practice socially appropriate eating skills and modify eating behaviors if necessary.	_____
☐	☐	Can evaluate environments for emotional safety and possible stressful events.	_____
☐	☐	Can stand in line and behave appropriately in a variety of situations (e.g., grocery store, movie, cafeteria).	_____

Goals/ Objectives Needed	Further Assessment Needed	Transition Knowledge and Skill Statements	Notes
☐	☐	Can evaluate personal behavior in light of specific setting and modify behavior if needed.	_____
☐	☐	Can be sensitive and responsive to social cues in verbal communication.	_____
☐	☐	Can perform basic social skills in daily situations (e.g., courtesy, sharing, cooperation).	_____
☐	☐	Can interpret nonverbal communicative social cues (e.g., gestures and body language) appropriately.	_____
☐	☐	Can understand that other individuals have different value systems, and then adjust own behavior appropriately.	_____
☐	☐	Can differentiate between when it is and when it is not appropriate to follow examples and practices of others in a group.	_____
☐	☐	Can understand and practice asking for and giving of favors.	_____
☐	☐	Can understand the limitations of friendship.	_____
☐	☐	Can initiate and return phone calls.	_____
		45. Possesses skills for getting along well with coworkers.	_____
☐	☐	Can practice basic social amenities in work situations (e.g., courtesy, sharing, taking turns).	_____
☐	☐	Knows the effects of prejudice and stereotyping in the work environment.	_____
☐	☐	Can be sensitive to others in the workplace.	_____
☐	☐	Can share with others at the workplace.	_____
☐	☐	Can show consideration of others at the workplace.	_____
☐	☐	Can react to rejection appropriately.	_____
☐	☐	Can identify when a personal and/or social problem arises in the workplace and identify someone to assist in the resolution of that problem.	_____
☐	☐	Can consider the backgrounds, environment, knowledge, and interests of others in the workplace and communicate appropriately.	_____
☐	☐	Can participate in cooperative relationships.	_____
☐	☐	Can participate in collaborative relationships.	_____
☐	☐	Can recognize when assistance in a work task is needed and ask for help from a coworker.	_____
☐	☐	Can respond appropriately when treated unfairly by a coworker.	_____

Goals/ Objectives Needed	Further Assessment Needed	Transition Knowledge and Skill Statements	Notes
☐	☐	Can develop and maintain friendships in the workplace.	
☐	☐	Can initiate or respond to social conversations in the workplace.	
☐	☐	Can contribute in group problem solving.	
☐	☐	Can allow another individual to mediate in a dispute with a coworker.	
		46. Possesses skills for getting along well with supervisor.	
☐	☐	Can recognize authority and respond appropriately.	
☐	☐	Can follow instructions from an authority figure.	
☐	☐	Can respond to redirection by an authority figure.	
☐	☐	Knows the impact getting along with supervisor has on performance reports and promotability.	
☐	☐	Knows about the role of personal hygiene in promoting positive relationship with supervisor.	
☐	☐	Can identify what type of interpersonal relationship is typically expected between an employee and a supervisor and how it differs from relationships with his or her peers.	
☐	☐	Can recognize when assistance in a work task is needed and ask for help from a supervisor.	
☐	☐	Can respond appropriately when treated unfairly by a supervisor.	
☐	☐	Can understand the impact of the "chain of command" and practice using it in a relationship with the supervisor.	
☐	☐	Can meet supervisor's expectations in performance.	
☐	☐	Can adjust to different styles of supervision.	
☐	☐	Can show respect in words and actions.	
☐	☐	Can align employment goals with employing company.	
☐	☐	Can appropriately request or advocate for "reasonable accommodations."	
☐	☐	Knows that a job hierarchy exists and knows of his or her own position in the hierarchy.	
☐	☐	Can show willingness and interest to attend professional development activities (and meetings) prescribed by supervisor.	

Section 3

Selected Informal Assessment Instruments for Transition

Contents

The following codes are provided to indicate who would likely complete the instrument:

T = Teacher
P = Parent/Guardian
S = Student

Employment

Further Education/Training

Note. Permission is granted to the user of this material to make unlimited copies of the forms in this section for teaching or clinical purposes.

Employment

Name: _____ Date: _____

THINGS THAT MAKE YOU SPECIAL

List 25 things that make you special. You might want to think about:

1. Your strengths
2. Things you know how to do well (your abilities/skills)
3. Things you enjoy doing
4. Things you have done of which you are proud
5. Your talents
6. Important things you have learned
7. Positive things about your personality

REMEMBER: YOU MUST HAVE 25 ITEMS ON YOUR LIST!

1. _____
2. _____
3. _____
4. _____
5. _____
6. _____
7. _____
8. _____
9. _____
10. _____
11. _____
12. _____
13. _____

14. _____
15. _____
16. _____
17. _____
18. _____
19. _____
20. _____
21. _____
22. _____
23. _____
24. _____
25. _____

Source: A Student's Guide to the Americans with Disabilities Act: Teacher's Resource Guide, by R. M. Balser, B. M. Harvey, and K. L. Rotroff, 1996, Portland: Department of Vocational Services, Maine Medical Center. Copyright 1996 by R. M. Balser, B. M. Harvey, and K. L. Rotroff. Reprinted with permission.

Name: _____ Date: _____

SKILLS

Directions: Put a check (✓) next to all the things you are good at. Then put a star (∗) next to the three things you do best.

I'm good at:

_____	Taking care of other people	_____	Reading
_____	Dealing with the public	_____	Writing
_____	Organizing things	_____	Math
_____	Making change	_____	Science
_____	Typing/filing	_____	Social studies
_____	Answering phones	_____	Art
_____	Using a computer	_____	Sports
_____	Waiting on tables	_____	Music
_____	Construction/carpentry	_____	Teaching
_____	Housepainting	_____	Baby-sitting
_____	Operating machines or tools	_____	Cooking
_____	Fixing machines	_____	Sewing or knitting
_____	Welding	_____	Cleaning
_____	Fixing cars	_____	Hairdressing
_____	Logging	_____	Driving
_____	Gardening	_____	Farming
_____	Yard work		

Use this space to list other things you do well:

_____   _____

_____   _____

_____   _____

_____   _____

_____   _____

Source: Speak Up for Yourself and Your Future, by K. F. Furney, N. Carlson, D. Lisi, S. Yuan, and L. Cravedi-Cheng, 1993, Burlington: University of Vermont. Copyright 1993 by University of Vermont. Reprinted with permission.

Name: _____ Date: _____

LIKES AND DISLIKES

Directions: Place a check (✓) next to any hobbies, interests, or activities that you like. Write "0" if you do not like the activity. Then put a star (∗) next to the three things you like to do the most and the three things you like least.

_____ Playing sports	_____ Drawing
_____ Camping, hiking	_____ Painting
_____ Fishing	_____ Taking care of people
_____ Hunting	_____ Baby-sitting
_____ Swimming	_____ Going to church
_____ Bicycling	_____ Belonging to a club
_____ Horseback riding	_____ Collecting things
_____ Skiing	_____ Visiting with friends
_____ Motorcycling	_____ Sleeping
_____ Keeping pets	_____ Food
_____ Raising animals	_____ Computers
_____ Gardening or taking care of plants	_____ Video games
_____ Farming	_____ Cooking
_____ Carpentry	_____ Sewing
_____ Fishing	_____ Knitting
_____ Beauty and hair care	_____ Reading
_____ Listening to music	_____ Photography
_____ Writing songs, stories, poems	_____ Four-wheelers
_____ Watching TV or movies	_____ Motocross
_____ Playing an instrument	_____ Working out

Use this space to add other hobbies or interests you can think of:

_____   _____

_____   _____

_____   _____

_____   _____

_____   _____

Source: Speak Up for Yourself and Your Future, by K. F. Furney, N. Carlson, D. Lisi, S. Yuan, and L. Cravedi-Cheng, 1993, Burlington: University of Vermont. Copyright 1993 by University of Vermont. Reprinted with permission.

Name: _____ Date: _____

PERSONAL STRENGTHS

Directions: Place a check (✓) next to any sentence that describes you. When you've finished put a star (∗) next to the three sentences that best describe you.

_____ I'm reliable.

_____ I'm friendly.

_____ I'm easy to get along with.

_____ I try to follow instructions.

_____ I like to do things with others.

_____ I like to do things on my own.

_____ I like to help other people.

_____ I like to keep things neat and

_____ organized.

_____ I like to have a good time.

_____ I don't brag too much.

_____ I stick with things until they get

_____ done.

_____ I can work out my problems on

_____ my own.

_____ I ask others for help when I need it.

_____ I can help others work out their

_____ problems.

_____ I'm good with mechanical things.

_____ I have good common sense.

_____ I am good at many things.

_____ I'm energetic.

_____ I'm a good listener.

_____ I'm polite.

_____ I'm honest.

_____ I'm hardworking.

_____ I'm usually on time.

_____ I'm serious

_____ I'm generous.

_____ I'm proud of myself.

_____ I can keep a secret.

_____ I'm a good friend.

_____ I'm a good student.

_____ I'm musical.

_____ I'm artistic

_____ I'm creative.

_____ I'm good with words.

_____ I can "get to the heart of things."

_____ I'm good with my hands.

_____ I am good at one or two things.

Use this space to write down your other strengths:

_____ _____

_____ _____

_____ _____

_____ _____

_____ _____

Source: Speak Up for Yourself and Your Future, by K. F. Furney, N. Carlson, D. Lisi, S. Yuan, and L. Cravedi-Cheng, 1993, Burlington: University of Vermont. Copyright 1993 by University of Vermont. Reprinted with permission.

51

Name: _____ Date: _____

Interest Inventory

Please fill in the blanks with your most honest answers.

1. When you have an hour or two to spend as you please, what do you like to do?
    _____

2. What games do you like to play? _____

3. What things have you made? _____

4. What tools or playthings do you have? _____

5. What do you collect? _____

6. What are your hobbies? _____

7. If you could have one wish that might come true, what would it be? _____
    _____

8. What is your favorite TV program? _____

9. Which movie have you liked best? _____

10. What is the best book you have ever read? _____

11. What kind of books do you like best? _____

12. What magazines do you read? _____

13. Have you read books or stories about the kind of work you want to do when you finish
    school? Name them: _____
    _____

14. Have you seen anyone on television or in the movies who does the kind of work you
    want to do? _____

15. What school subject do you like best? _____

16. What school subject do you like least? _____

Source: Connections: A Transition Curriculum for Grades 3 Through 6, by Jefferson County Public Schools, n.d., Denver, CO: Author.
Copyright by Jefferson County Public Schools. Reprinted with permission.

Name: _____ Date: _____

Who Am I?

What are you all about? Answer the questions below to help you find out.

1. What do you like to do with your spare time? _____
   _____

2. Where would you like to go on a vacation? _____
   _____

3. If you could change your name, what would it be? _____
   _____

4. What is your favorite video? _____
   _____

5. What do you think you're best at? _____
   _____

6. What movie do you like seeing over and over again? _____
   _____

7. What pet would you like to have? _____
   _____

8. What famous person would you like to meet? _____
   _____

9. What possession of yours are you most proud of? _____
   _____

10. Choose one idea from the ideas above and tell more about your feelings on the lines below.

   _____
   _____
   _____
   _____
   _____

Source: Connections: A Transition Curriculum for Grades 3 Through 6, by Jefferson County Public Schools, n.d., Denver, CO: Author.
Copyright by Jefferson County Public Schools. Reprinted with permission.

Name: _____ Date: _____

Age: _____

My Interests Review

1. I liked these things when

    I was little: a. _____

                      b. _____

    Now: a. _____

                      b. _____

2. I was interested in these things when

    I was little: a. _____

                      b. _____

    Now   a. _____

                      b. _____

3. I wanted to be these things when

    I was little: a. _____

                      b. _____

4. When I grow up, I might want to be

    a. _____

    b. _____

    c. _____

Source: Connections: A Transition Curriculum for Grades 3 Through 6, by Jefferson County Public Schools, n.d., Denver, CO: Author. Copyright by Jefferson County Public Schools. Reprinted with permission.

Name: _____ Date: _____

What's My Bag?

Please place a check mark next to the choice that seems to be most like you.

1. _____ work indoors
   _____ work outdoors

2. _____ work alone
   _____ work with other people

3. _____ work with your hands
   _____ work with your mind

4. _____ work in the daytime
   _____ work at night

5. _____ work for a boss
   _____ be a boss yourself

6. _____ create or build something
   _____ use plans someone else has made

7. _____ work in a city
   _____ work in the country

8. _____ make a lot of money at a job you don't like
   _____ enjoy your job

9. _____ have a job you can get when you finish high school
   _____ have a job that requires college

10. _____ have a job where you travel
    _____ have a job where you stay in one place

11. _____ work in your own home
    _____ work outside your home

12. _____ be famous
    _____ be known only to your friends and family

13. _____ have a job where you help other people
    _____ have a job where you work more with machines, papers, and other things

Look carefully at the choices you have made. Think of three jobs you might one day have that would interest you most.

1. _____

2. _____

3. _____

Source: Connections: A Transition Curriculum for Grades 3 Through 6, by Jefferson County Public Schools, n.d., Denver, CO: Author.
Copyright by Jefferson County Public Schools. Reprinted with permission.

Name: _____ Date: _____

This Is How I See Myself

Please check your choice for each of the following. You may need some help understanding what these phrases really mean; ask your teacher!

Behavior	High	So-So	Low
I am patient	☐	☐	☐
I know when to keep quiet	☐	☐	☐
I am a risk-taker	☐	☐	☐
I am an activity-starter	☐	☐	☐
I can do constructive arguing	☐	☐	☐
I can communicate effectively	☐	☐	☐
I am calm	☐	☐	☐
I am a good follower	☐	☐	☐

Possible Job Interests	High	So-So	Low
Building services (planning, construction, maintenance, etc.)	☐	☐	☐
Mechanical and industrial (engineer, mechanic, shop supervisor, etc.)	☐	☐	☐
Personal services (counselor, lawyer, teacher, etc.)	☐	☐	☐
Clerical and sales (secretary, clerk, computer operator, etc.)	☐	☐	☐
Medical (doctor, therapist)	☐	☐	☐
Hospitality, food (chef, hotel, etc.)	☐	☐	☐
Outdoors (plants and animals)	☐	☐	☐
Creative arts (author, painter, actor, etc.)	☐	☐	☐
Scientific (chemist, physicist, geologist, etc.)	☐	☐	☐

The Kind of Job I'd Like

	High	So-So	Low
Work under pressure	☐	☐	☐
Like to meet deadlines	☐	☐	☐
Work with plants or animals	☐	☐	☐
Work with people	☐	☐	☐
Work with machines	☐	☐	☐
Sell products	☐	☐	☐
Sell ideas	☐	☐	☐
Take responsibility	☐	☐	☐
Regular hours	☐	☐	☐
Travel	☐	☐	☐
Help others	☐	☐	☐
Use math	☐	☐	☐
Use reading	☐	☐	☐

Problem Areas	**Many Problems**	**Some Problems**	**Few Problems**
Home	☐	☐	☐
Friends	☐	☐	☐
School work	☐	☐	☐
Personal	☐	☐	☐

Source: *Connections: A Transition Curriculum for Grades 3 Through 6,* by Jefferson County Public Schools, n.d., Denver, CO: Author. Copyright by Jefferson County Public Schools. Reprinted with permission.

Name: _____ Date: _____

What Can I Do?
Personal Profile

Wow! Look at all these skills I already have that will help me now and in the future.

<u>Here's a list of my strengths:</u>
(Remember to list anything and everything you do well that will help you do a good job in school or on a job.)

_____

_____

_____

_____

_____

_____

_____

_____

_____

_____

<u>Here's a list of those skills I'd like to use on the job:</u>

_____

_____

_____

_____

_____

_____

_____

_____

_____

_____

Everyone has some areas that could use improvement. These are the areas I would like to work on:

_____

_____

_____

_____

_____

_____

Source: Connections: A Transition Curriculum for Grades 3 Through 6, by Jefferson County Public Schools, n.d., Denver, CO: Author. Copyright by Jefferson County Public Schools. Reprinted with permission.

Assessing My Multiple Intelligences

INSTRUCTIONS: Complete each sentence below by filling in the blank with the number that best indicates your **degree of expertise** in each. Enter the number in the blank before the statement. Total the score for each intelligence in the box at the bottom of the column.

4 exceptional expertise	3 high expertise	2 moderate expertise	1 minimal expertise	0 no expertise

$2A(B)=C^2$

Verbal/Linguistic

— I read and understand what I've read with—

— I listen to the radio or a spoken-word cassette and understand with—

— I play word games like Scrabble, Anagrams, or Password with—

— I make up tongue twisters, nonsense rhymes, or puns with—

— I use words in writing or speaking with—

— In my English, social studies, and history courses in school, I displayed—

— Others have recognized that my writing shows—

— I often convince others to agree with me with—

— I speak in public with—

— I use words to create mental pictures with—

☐ Total

Logical/Mathematical

— I compute numbers in my head with—

— In my math and/or science courses in school, I displayed—

— I play games or solve brainteasers that require logical thinking with—

— I identify regularities or logical sequences in things with—

— I think in clear, abstract concepts with—

— I find logical flaws in things that people say and do with—

— I categorize and analyze information with—

— I piece together patterns from separate pieces of information with—

— I use symbols to manipulate data with—

— Others have recognized that my deductive ability shows—

☐ Total

Visual/Spatial

— I am able to use color with—

— I use a camera or camcorder to record what I see around me with—

— I do jigsaw puzzles, mazes, and other visual puzzles with—

— I format and layout publications with—

— I find my way around unfamiliar territory with—

— I draw or paint with—

— In Geometry classes in school, I displayed—

— I understand what a shape will look like when viewing it from directly above with—

— I design interior or exterior spaces with—

— I recognize shapes regardless of the angle from which I view them with—

☐ Total

Bodily/Kinesthetic

— I play tennis, golf, swim, or engage in some similar physical activity with—

— I sew, weave, or engage in some similar creative activity with—

— I build models, do woodworking, or construct things with—

— In activities or courses requiring physical or manual dexterity in school, I display—

— I use gestures or other forms of body language to convey ideas with—

— My physical coordination displays—

— I dance with—

— I express my feelings through physical activity with—

— I am recognized as having physical or manual abilities that exhibit—

— My dramatic ability shows—

☐ Total

59

(continues)

Assessing My Multiple Intelligences

INSTRUCTIONS: Complete each sentence below by filling in the blank with the number that best indicates your **degree of expertise** in each. Enter the number in the blank before the statement. Total the score for each intelligence in the box at the bottom of the column.

4	3	2	1	0
exceptional expertise	high expertise	moderate expertise	minimal expertise	no expertise

Musical

— I sing with—
— I can tell when a musical note is off-key with—
— I can sight read and sing or play a difficult musical piece with—
— I play a musical instrument with—
— I can hear a melody once and reproduce it with—
— I reproduce or create intricate rhythms with—
— I create new musical compositions with—
— I am recognized by others as having musical talent with—
— I direct others in creating musical selections with—
— I "hear" the patterns of relationships within a musical piece with—

☐ Total

Interpersonal

— I provide advice or counsel to others with—
— My ability to facilitate group work shows—
— I make friends with—
— I play social games such as Pictionary or Charades with—
— When teaching another person or groups of people, I display—
— In leading others, I exhibit—
— My involvement in social activities connected with my work, church, or community displays—
— I am able to understand the needs and emotions of others with—
— I work together with others to achieve a common goal with—
— I sense other people's motives or hidden agendas with—

☐ Total

Intrapersonal/ Introspective

— I reflect on ideas or events with—
— I achieve personal growth by using new information with—
— I achieve a resilience to setbacks with—
— I have developed a special hobby or interest with—
— I set important goals for my life with—
— I recognize my strengths and weaknesses (borne out by feedback from other sources) with—
— I use solitude to strengthen my inner resources with—
— I am strong willed or independent minded to a degree that exhibits—
— I keep a personal diary or journal to record the events of my inner life in a way that displays—
— I seek to understand my own motivation with—

☐ Total

Naturalist

— I can see variations in leaves with—
— I am able to identify a wide variety of insects, birds, or rocks with—
— Using a microscope, I can see very small differences between plants or animals with—
— I can identify the tracks and spoors of an animal with—
— I am able to tell the difference between harmless and poisonous plants or animals with—
— Using a telescope, I am able to identify stars, planets, and galaxies with—
— I can plan an attractive garden that has color during all four seasons of the year with—
— I am able to work with animals with—
— I am able to classify such things as rocks or aquatic life or clouds with—
— I am able to grow plants with—

☐ Total

Source: Assessing My Multiple Intelligences, by National Dropout Prevention Center at Clemson University, 1995, Clemson, SC: Author. Copyright 1995 by the National Dropout Prevention Center. Reprinted with permission.

Name: _____ Date: _____

Grade: _____ (7th–9th) Rater: _____

Exploration Phase:
Career Education Checklist

Enter the date of evaluation in the boxes at the right.

	Seldom	Sometimes	Most of the Time
Self			
1. Can express his/her personal interests			
2. Knows how s/he feels about him/herself and how this affects him/her			
3. Aware of physical strengths and abilities			
Interpersonal Relations			
1. Displays appropriate emotional characteristics when interacting with others			
2. Knows what others think of him/her			
3. Understands and appreciates different characteristics in different people			
4. Knows that one will interact in different groups in different situations			
Self and Society			
1. Able to verbalize his/her own personal values			
2. Understands that people need to work if society is to survive			
3. Understands that the world is changing and jobs are changing			
Decision Making			
1. Has some long-term goals regarding a career			
2. Knows his/herabilities, qualities, values, and hopes			
3. Takes responsibility for his/her decisions			
4. Matches his/her personal characteristics with possible career choices			
5. Understands what s/he needs to know for various career choices			

(continues)

	Seldom	Sometimes	Most of the Time
Economics			
1. Knows difference between consumers and producers			
2. Understands how supply and demand affects work world			
3. Understands how world of work (income, hours, etc.) affects lifestyle of individuals			
4. Understands the concept of fringe benefits, insurance, etc.			
5. Understands minimum wage and hour laws, social security, and federal and state income tax			
Occupational Knowledge			
1. Knows how to use education as aid in developing skills for occupations			
2. Explores a wide range of occupations			
3. Knows what skills and education are needed for various jobs			
4. Knows general concept of what needs to be done to advance in various jobs			
5. Understands various working conditions with various jobs			
6. Understands role of employer, employee, manager, etc.			
7. Understands law of supply and demand as it applies to obtaining a job			
8. Understands how to seek employment			
Work Attitudes and Behaviors			
1. Displays behavior appropriate for school and community			
2. Understands how working at a job integrates one into the community			
3. Understands that personal satisfaction is gained from work and leisure			
4. Understands that social recognition is related to work			
5. Understands monetary rewards come from work			
6. Understands that one may change jobs as one gets older and matures			

Source: Career/Transition Planning Forms, Area 4, by Area Education Agency 4, n.d., Sioux Center, IA: Author. Copyright by Area Education Agency 4. Reprinted with permission.

Name: _____ Date: _____

Career Portfolio

Directions: Evaluate the student, using the rating scale on the right. Circle the appropriate number to indicate the degree of competency. The rating for each of the tasks should reflect job readiness rather than the grade given in the class.

EMPLOYABILITY SKILLS (Competencies that will enable the individual to obtain and retain a job)

The student can: **SCALE**

1. Establish realistic career goals/choices	N 1 2 3 4
2. Display a positive attitude toward work (work ethic)	N 1 2 3 4
3. Demonstrate a good record of attendance	N 1 2 3 4
4. Display punctuality at school, work, and following breaks	N 1 2 3 4
5. Display a pride in work	N 1 2 3 4
6. Demonstrate honesty	N 1 2 3 4
7. Demonstrate dependability	N 1 2 3 4
8. Observe and follow classroom/work rules and regulations	N 1 2 3 4
9. Display initiative (e.g., begin work without being asked, assume additional responsibility, help others voluntarily)	N 1 2 3 4
10. Work at a consistent pace	N 1 2 3 4
11. Manage time appropriately	N 1 2 3 4
12. Demonstrate work stability (remains on the job/task until completed)	N 1 2 3 4
13. Work effectively under pressure or within time limits	N 1 2 3 4
14. Keep work area clean	N 1 2 3 4
15. Display respect for other people	N 1 2 3 4
16. Show respect for property of others	N 1 2 3 4
17. Seek help when needed	N 1 2 3 4
18. React appropriately to constructive criticism	N 1 2 3 4
19. Accept praise appropriately	N 1 2 3 4
20. Assume responsibility for own actions/behaviors	N 1 2 3 4
21. Demonstrate appropriate reactions to own mistakes (e.g., acceptance, correction)	N 1 2 3 4
22. Demonstrate appropriate problem-solving skills (e.g., identify problem, list possible solutions, select a solution, evaluate results)	N 1 2 3 4
23. Demonstrate willingness to learn new skills/information	N 1 2 3 4
24. Demonstrate adaptability to changing situations	N 1 2 3 4
25. Follow safety regulations	N 1 2 3 4
26. Respond appropriately to classroom and/or job related emergencies	N 1 2 3 4
27. Practice good hygiene/grooming	N 1 2 3 4
28. Dress appropriately for work/specific job	N 1 2 3 4
29. Correctly complete a job application	N 1 2 3 4
30. Demonstrate appropriate job interviewing skills	N 1 2 3 4
31. Demonstrate the ability to complete a job resumé	N 1 2 3 4

Source: "Transition Planning: Developing a Career Portfolio for Students with Disabilities," by M. Sarkees-Wircenski and J. L. Wircenski, 1994, *Career Development for Exceptional Individuals, 17*(2), p. 208. Copyright 1994 by Division on Career Development and Transition, the Council for Exceptional Children. Reprinted with permission.

Name: _____ Date: _____

Job-Related Interest and Preference Inventory

1. What job(s) would you like to have when you finish school? _____
   _____

   Why? Have you done this job before? _____
   _____

2. What are your favorite days of the week to work? _____
   _____

   Why? _____
   _____

3. What hours or time of the day do you want to work? _____
   _____

4. Are you willing to work nights or weekends, if the boss asks you to? _____
   _____

5. Do you want to work indoors or outdoors? _____
   _____

6. Would you rather be standing or sitting at work? _____
   _____

7. Do you want to work alone or with other people? _____
   _____

8. Do you want to work at a fast-paced and busy place or at a slow place? _____
   _____

9. Do you like it to be noisy or quiet when you work? _____
   _____

10. Do you prefer music or no music playing where you work? _____
    _____

11. Do you prefer a job that makes you wear a uniform? _____
    _____

12. Do you want a job that requires you to dress up in nice clothes for work? _____

_____

13. Do you prefer to work for a business with a lot of employees or with just a few

employees? _____

14. What kind of setting(s) do you want to work in?
    - ☐ hospital   ☐ outdoors   ☐ stock room   ☐ animals   ☐ home   ☐ business
    - ☐ farm   ☐ hotel   ☐ office   ☐ store front   ☐ water   ☐ cubicle
    - ☐ shopping mall

15. How far/long are you willing to travel to get to work? _____

_____

16. How much money would you like to make at a job? _____

_____

17. What else are you looking for in a job? What does the job have to have? _____

_____

18. What are your favorite places to go in the community? _____

_____

19. What are your favorite subjects at school? _____

_____

Why? _____

_____

Name: _____ Date: _____

Getting Ready for Your Job:
A Job Preparation Awareness Survey

Type of job I would like to have when I finish school: _____

Please mark the best answer below:

	Yes	No	Don't Know Yet
1. Are there certain high school classes that would help you prepare for this job?	☐	☐	☐
2. Is there training that you will need to get (outside of school) in order to get this job?	☐	☐	☐
3. Will you need to go to a vocational school or to college to prepare yourself for this job?	☐	☐	☐
4. Are you taking the high school classes that you need to take if you are going to college?	☐	☐	☐
5. Do you know how hard or easy it will be to get this job? (e.g., Do a lot of people apply for this type of job? How many positions exist?)	☐	☐	☐
6. Will you have to move to another town/city to get this job?	☐	☐	☐
7. Do you know how much money this job usually pays?	☐	☐	☐
8. Do you know where to go to find out more about this job?	☐	☐	☐
9. Do you know anyone who does this job?	☐	☐	☐

Name of client: _____

Name of rater: _____

Date: _____

WORK PERSONALITY PROFILE

Please describe the client's observed work performance using the five options listed below to complete the 58 behavioral items.

4 = a definite strength, an employability asset

3 = adequate performance, not a particular strength

2 = performance inconsistent, potentially an employability problem

1 = a problem area, will definitely limit the person's chances for employment

X = no opportunity to observe the behavior

1. _____ Sufficiently alert and aware

2. _____ Learns new assignments quickly

3. _____ Works steadily during entire work period

4. _____ Accepts changes in work assignments

5. _____ Needs virtually no direct supervision

6. _____ Requests help in an appropriate fashion

7. _____ Approaches supervisory personnel with confidence

8. _____ Is appropriately friendly with supervisor

9. _____ Shows pride in group effort

10. _____ Shows interest in what others are doing

11. _____ Expresses likes and dislikes appropriately

12. _____ Initiates work-related activities on time

13. _____ Accepts work assignments with instructions from supervisor without arguing

14. _____ Improves performance when shown how

15. _____ Works at routine jobs without resistance

16. _____ Expresses willingness to try new assignments

17. _____ Carries out assigned tasks without prompting

18. _____ Asks for further instructions if task is not clear

19. _____ Accepts correction without becoming upset

20. _____ Discusses personal problems with supervisor only if work related

21. _____ Accepts assignment to group tasks

22. _____ Seeks out coworkers to be friends

23. _____ Responds when others initiate conversation

24. _____ Conforms to rules and regulations

25. _____ Maintains satisfactory personal hygiene habits

26. _____ Changes work methods when instructed to do so

27. _____ Pays attention to details while working

28. _____ Maintains productivity despite change in routine

29. _____ Recognizes own mistakes

30. _____ Asks for help when having difficulty with tasks

31. _____ Comfortable with supervisor

32. _____ Gets along with staff

33. _____ Works comfortably in group tasks

34. _____ Appears comfortable in social interactions

35. _____ Initiates conversations with others

36. _____ Displays good judgment in use of obscenities and vulgarities

37. _____ Arrives appropriately dressed for work

38. _____ Maintains improved work procedures after correction

39. _____ Maintains work pace even if distractions occur

40. _____ Performs satisfactorily in tasks that require variety and change

41. _____ Initiates action to correct own mistakes

42. _____ Performance remains stable in supervisor's presence

43. _____ Supportive of others in group tasks

44. _____ Joins social groups when they are available

45. _____ Listens while other person speaks, avoids interrupting

46. _____ Expresses pleasure in accomplishment

47. _____ Listens to instructions or corrections attentively

48. _____ Moves from job to job easily

49. _____ Needs less than average amount of supervision

50. _____ Offers assistance to coworkers when appropriate

51. _____ Is sought out frequently by coworkers

52. _____ Expresses positive feelings, such as praise, liking for others

53. _____ Displays good judgment in playing practical jokes or "horsing around"

54. _____ Transfers previously learned skills to new task

55. _____ Handles problems with only occasional help

56. _____ Assumes assigned role in group tasks

57. _____ Expresses negative feelings appropriately, such as anger, fear, sadness

58. _____ Controls temper

Source: "The Work Personality Profile," by R. T. Roessler and B. Bolton, 1986, *Vocational Evaluation and Work Adjustment Bulletin,* *18*(1), pp. 8–11. Copyright 1986 by Vocational Evaluation and Work Adjustment Bulletin. Reprinted with permission.

Employability/Life Skills Assessment
(Ages 14–21 years)

STUDENT INFORMATION

Name: _____ Birthdate: _____

RATIONALE

Employability skills are those personal social behaviors and daily living habits that have been identified by employers and young entry-level workers as essential for obtaining employment and for success in the workplace. These are life skills that must be taught with the same rigor as basic skills. The development of such skills is a lifelong process, with performance being relative to a student's ability and age. Teachers at all age levels have the responsibility to teach employability skills.

GENERAL DIRECTIONS

This criterion-referenced checklist may be used yearly, beginning at the age of 14, to assess a student's level of performance in the 24 critical employability skill areas identified by Ohio's Employability Skills Project. Three descriptors are provided for each skill. **Student performance should be rated using the following scale: 3 = usually, 2 = sometimes, 1 = seldom, 0 = never.**

EXAMPLE (for a 14-year-old student)

I. SELF-HELP SKILLS

A. Demonstrates personal hygiene and grooming by:
—meeting parent expectation for cleanliness.
—meeting parent expectation for good grooming (hair combed, shirt tucked in, etc.).
—meeting parent expectation for consistent, independent personal hygiene and grooming.

AGE	14	15	16	17	18	19	20	21
	2							
	1							
	1							
T	4							

B. Dresses appropriately by:
—choosing and wearing clothes that are appropriate for the weather/activity/social custom.
—identifying when clothes should not be worn (dirty, ill fitting, etc.).
—wearing clothes that are in good condition, clean and pressed with detail given to appearance.

AGE	14	15	16	17	18	19	20	21
	2							
	3							
	1							
T	6							

Scores for each descriptor are added, providing a value that can be recorded on the Student Profile of Employability Skills. When completed, the profile yields a graphic representation of employability skills performance that will help in planning instruction.

(continues)

Employability/Life Skills Assessment *(Continued)*

Key: 3 = Usually, 2 = Sometimes, 1 = Seldom, 0 = Never

I. SELF-HELP SKILLS

A. Demonstrates personal hygiene and grooming by:

—meeting teacher expectation for cleanliness.

—meeting teacher expectation for good grooming (hair combed, shirt tucked in, etc.).

—meeting teacher expectation for consistent, independent personal hygiene and grooming.

AGE	14	15	16	17	18	19	20	21
T								

B. Dresses appropriately by:

—choosing and wearing clothes that are appropriate for the weather/activity/social custom.

—identifying when clothes should not be worn (dirty, ill fitting, etc.).

—wearing clothes that are in good condition, clean and pressed with detail given to appearance.

C. Travels independently by:

—walking or riding to school following safety rules.

—getting around the school building and grounds.

—getting around the community.

D. Communicates effectively by:

—demonstrating effective listening skills, including eye contact.

—expressing self, answering and asking questions.

—demonstrating expected conversational skills (turn talking, choice of appropriate topic, etc.).

II. GENERAL WORK HABITS

A. Attends regularly/arrives on time by:

—having no unexcused absences.

—arriving at class, school, or work on time.

—following school procedures when tardy or absent.

B. Stays on task by:

—meeting teacher expectations regarding length of time on task.

—completing a task without being distracted.

—returning to work if distracted.

C. Works independently by:

—locating materials.

—beginning work promptly.

—asking peers/teachers questions about a given task at the appropriate time.

AGE	14	15	16	17	18	19	20	21
T								

III. TASK RELATED SKILLS

A. Cares for tools, materials, and work area by:

—meeting expectations for the use of tools and materials (scissors, paste, screwdriver, etc.).

—locating and returning tools to the proper storage area.

—maintaining a clean work area.

B. Practices safety rules by:

—stating and using safety rules appropriate to grade level and situation.

—using tools and materials only for their specified purpose.

—demonstrating correct safety procedures in simulated emergency situations.

IV. QUANTITY OF WORK

A. Completes work on time by:

—completing work on time with teacher prompts.

—completing work on time without teacher prompts.

—working at an acceptable speed for a given task.

B. Exhibits stamina by:

—finishing age-appropriate tasks without a break.

—maintaining an acceptable level of speed without tiring.

—completing new tasks without diminishing the level of performance of former tasks.

C. Adapts to increased demands in workload by:

—responding to additional tasks with teacher prompts.

—attempting new tasks without demonstrating frustration.

—responding to additional tasks without teacher prompts.

Employability/Life Skills Assessment *(Continued)*

> **Key:** 3 = Usually, 2 = Sometimes, 1 = Seldom, 0 = Never

V. QUALITY OF WORK

AGE

A. Makes appropriate choices and decisions by:

—choosing an appropriate solution when given options.

—making age-appropriate decisions with teacher intervention.

—responding to a problem situation with reasonable alternative solutions.

	14	15	16	17	18	19	20	21
T								

B. Recognizes and corrects mistakes by:

—examining work for errors before submitting it.

—using self-check methods to evaluate work.

—making corrections once an error has been identified.

VI. RELATIONSHIP TO SUPERVISOR/ TEACHER

	14	15	16	17	18	19	20	21
T								

A. Accepts constructive criticism from supervisor/teacher by:

—listening to constructive criticism without making inappropriate gestures or comments.

—making specified changes based on constructive criticism.

—identifying that changes have been made and that performance has improved.

	14	15	16	17	18	19	20	21
T								

B. Follows directions from supervisor/ teacher by:

—correctly completing tasks following verbal directions.

—correctly completing tasks following written directions.

—communicating and accepting consequences for not following directions.

	14	15	16	17	18	19	20	21
T								

C. Seeks help when needed by:

—identifying when help is needed.

—asking for assistance when help is needed.

—using requested information to remedy the problem.

	14	15	16	17	18	19	20	21
T								

VII. RELATIONSHIP TO PEERS

A. Works cooperatively with peers by:

—working well with others.

—seeking help from coworkers.

—directing coworkers without being overbearing.

	14	15	16	17	18	19	20	21
T								

B. Shows respect for the rights and property of others by:

—taking turns.

—asking permission to use another's property.

—treating borrowed property with respect.

AGE

	14	15	16	17	18	19	20	21
T								

C. Uses appropriate language and manners with peers by:

—using everyday manners (please, thank you).

—avoiding teasing/ridiculing others.

—using language appropriate for a given situation.

	14	15	16	17	18	19	20	21
T								

VIII. WORK ATTITUDES

A. Develops and seeks personal goals by:

—demonstrating short term personal goals such as completing daily work.

—explaining planned activities for after school, weekend, or vacation.

—seeking and developing personal goals that are viable and consistent with abilities and limitations.

T								

B. Shows initiative by:

—beginning a task as soon as requested to do so.

—beginning a task without prompting.

—asking for additional work or directions once a task is completed.

T								

C. Accepts societal values and rewards by:

—acknowledging various types of rewards for work well done (stickers, free time, etc.).

—recognizing when good work has been done.

—responding appropriately when praised for doing a good job.

T								

D. Takes pride in working by:

—sharing accomplishments with others (takes papers home, collects stickers, responds to point systems/grades).

—working for positions requiring improvement in skills.

—contributing to the common good of the group.

T								

(continues)

Student Profile of Employability Skills

SCORE	SELF-HELP SKILLS					WORK HABITS			TASK RELATED		WORK QUANTITY			WORK QUALITY		RELATIONS: SUPERVISOR			RELATIONS: PEERS		WORK ATTITUDES					SCORE	AGE
	HYGIENE, GROOMING	DRESSES APPROPRIATELY	TRAVELS INDEPENDENTLY	COMMUNICATES EFFECTIVELY		ATTENDS, ON TIME	STAYS ON TASK	WORKS INDEPENDENTLY	CARES FOR TOOLS, ETC.	PRACTICES SAFETY	COMPLETES WORK	EXHIBITS STAMINA	ADAPTS TO DEMANDS	CHOICES, DECISIONS	CORRECTS MISTAKES	ACCEPTS CRITICISM	FOLLOWS DIRECTIONS	SEEKS HELP	WORKS COOPERATIVELY	SHOWS RESPECT	LANGUAGE, MANNERS	PERSONAL GOALS	SHOWS INITIATIVE	VALUES, REWARDS	PRIDE IN WORK		

Age rows (each with scores 9 8 7 6 5 4 3 2 1 0):

- 14 YEARS — Completed by ___ / Date Administered ___
- 15 YEARS — Completed by ___ / Date Administered ___
- 16 YEARS — Completed by ___ / Date Administered ___
- 17 YEARS — Completed by ___ / Date Administered ___
- 18 YEARS — Completed by ___ / Date Administered ___
- 19 YEARS — Completed by ___ / Date Administered ___
- 20 YEARS — Completed by ___ / Date Administered ___
- 21 YEARS — Completed by ___ / Date Administered ___

Source: *Employability/Life Skills Assessment: Ages 14–21,* by R. Weaver and J. R. DeLuca, 1987, Dayton, OH: Miami Valley Special Education Center and Montgomery County Board of Education. Copyright by R. Weaver and J. R. DeLuca. Reprinted with permission.

Individual Supports Assessment Form

Date: _____ Provider ID: _____

Consumer Name: _____ Employment Specialist: _____

SS#: _____ ID Code: _____

Street: _____ Initial: _____

City, State, Zip: _____ On-Going: _____

Please answer each question regarding the consumer's current goals, preferences, and experiences. Information needed to respond to each question should be obtained from the consumer during a face-to-face interview prior to placement into employment or while working if a change in his or her employment situation is desired.

I. Vocational Goals and Experience

1. What are your career and life goals? (Describe the job or position you would like to have and any other goals you would like to pursue, e.g., school, independent living, etc.)

   _____

   _____

   _____

   _____

   _____

2. Where might you like to work? (check all that apply)

   _____ 1) restaurant
   _____ 2) grocery store
   _____ 3) retail store
   _____ 4) hospital/nursing home
   _____ 5) office building
   _____ 6) hotel/motel
   _____ 7) university/school
   _____ 8) day-care facility
   _____ 9) factory
   _____ 10) service provider/agency (e.g., church, park)
   _____ 11) don't know
   _____ 12) other (Describe: _____)

3. a. What type of job might you like to have? (check all that apply)

   _____ 1) dishwasher/kitchen utility worker
   _____ 2) food prep person
   _____ 3) food server
   _____ 4) bus person/lobby attendant
   _____ 5) janitor/housekeeper

(continues)

_____ 6) laborer

_____ 7) assembler

_____ 8) laundry worker

_____ 9) stock clerk/bagger/warehouse worker

_____ 10) machine operator

_____ 11) clerical/office worker

_____ 12) groundskeeper/landscaper

_____ 13) human service worker

_____ 14) don't know

_____ 15) other (Describe: _____)

b. Is there anyone you know who works in the places or in a position that you might like to have that you wouldn't mind us contacting?

NAME	RELATIONSHIP	PHONE #	EMPLOYMENT

4. What types of things might be important to you in working in the position of your choice? (check all that apply)

_____ 1) hours

_____ 2) benefits (e.g., paid vacations, sick leave, employee discount)

_____ 3) health insurance

_____ 4) wages

_____ 5) location of business

_____ 6) coworkers

_____ 7) work environment

_____ 8) nothing/don't know

_____ 9) other (Describe: _____)

5. Have you ever been employed in a paid job before?

_____ 1) yes

_____ 2) no

If yes, a) where did you work?   1) _____

2) _____

3) _____

b) What was your job title?   1) _____

2) _____

3) _____

6. Have you participated in any other work experiences (e.g., volunteer work, vocational training, etc.)?

     _____   1) yes

     _____   2) no

If yes, describe the work that you did. _____

_____

7. Who might you like to assist you in finding a job? (check all that apply)

     _____   1) parents

     _____   2) brother/sister

     _____   3) relatives

     _____   4) girlfriend/boyfriend/spouse

     _____   5) friends

     _____   6) community member (Describe: _____)

     _____   7) professional (Describe: _____)

     _____   8) no one/don't know

     _____   9) other (Describe: _____)

8. In what ways would you be willing to help with finding a job? (check all that apply)

     _____   1) identifying job leads

     _____   2) looking at the newspaper

     _____   3) contacting employers

     _____   4) picking up job applications

     _____   5) developing a resumé

     _____   6) none/don't know

     _____   7) other (Describe: _____)

9. What means of transportation would you be willing to use in order to go to and from work? (check all that apply)

     _____   1) drive self

     _____   2) friend or family member transport

     _____   3) walk

     _____   4) ride a bicycle

     _____   5) ride the bus

     _____   6) use a taxi

     _____   7) carpool

     _____   8) ride with coworkers

     _____   9) use specialized transportation

     _____   10) none/don't know

     _____   11) other (Describe: _____)

(continues)

II. Interests

10. What do you do during your free time? (check all that apply)

_____ 1) watch television
_____ 2) shop/go to the mall
_____ 3) participate in organized recreational or sporting activities
_____ 4) go to sporting events
_____ 5) go bowling
_____ 6) roller-skate/ice-skate
_____ 7) read books or magazines
_____ 8) go to movies
_____ 9) listen to music
_____ 10) go to concerts
_____ 11) hang out with friends
_____ 12) go dancing
_____ 13) talk on the telephone
_____ 14) hobbies
_____ 15) arts and crafts
_____ 16) nothing
_____ 17) other (Describe: _____)

11. Are there other things you would like to do during your free time?

_____ 1) yes
_____ 2) no

If yes, what kinds of things would you like to do? (check all that apply)

_____ 1) watch television
_____ 2) shop/go to the mall
_____ 3) participate in organized recreational or sporting activities
_____ 4) go to sporting events
_____ 5) go bowling
_____ 6) roller-skate/ice-skate
_____ 7) read books or magazines
_____ 8) go to movies
_____ 9) listen to music
_____ 10) go to concerts
_____ 11) hang out with friends
_____ 12) go dancing
_____ 13) talk on the telephone
_____ 14) hobbies
_____ 15) arts and crafts
_____ 16) other (Describe: _____)

12. Who do you usually spend your free time with? (check all that apply)

   _____   1) friends

   _____   2) girlfriend/boyfriend/spouse

   _____   3) parents

   _____   4) brothers/sisters

   _____   5) relatives

   _____   6) neighbors

   _____   7) peers (e.g., students, workshop participants)

   _____   8) general public

   _____   9) no one

   _____   10) other (Describe: _____)

13. Do you participate in any clubs or organizations? (check all that apply)

   _____   1) 4-H clubs

   _____   2) church/synagogue

   _____   3) health/fitness club

   _____   4) hobby clubs (e.g., card or stamp collecting, bingo, etc.)

   _____   5) community recreational programs

   _____   6) sports teams

   _____   7) school clubs/groups

   _____   8) YMCA/YWCA

   _____   9) civic organizations (Describe: _____)

   _____   10) special interest groups (Describe: _____)

   _____   11) none/don't know

   _____   12) other (Describe: _____)

14. Are there any clubs or organizations you would like to belong to or participate in?

   _____   1) yes

   _____   2) no

If yes, what clubs or organizations would you like to become involved with? (check all that apply)

   _____   1) 4-H clubs

   _____   2) church/synagogue

   _____   3) health/fitness club

   _____   4) hobby clubs (e.g., card or stamp collecting, bingo, etc.)

   _____   5) community recreational programs

   _____   6) sports teams

   _____   7) school clubs/groups

   _____   8) YMCA/YWCA

   _____   9) civic organizations (Describe: _____)

   _____   10) special interest groups (Describe: _____)

   _____   11) other (Describe: _____)

(continues)

15. a. Does a family member or friend belong to or participate in any of the following clubs or organizations? (check all that apply)

_____ 1) American Association of Retired Citizens
_____ 2) American Red Cross
_____ 3) Big Brothers/Big Sisters
_____ 4) Chamber of Commerce
_____ 5) church/synagogue
_____ 6) Civitans
_____ 7) community or neighborhood association
_____ 8) Cooperative Extension Service
_____ 9) Elks Club
_____ 10) hobby clubs
_____ 11) Jaycees
_____ 12) Junior League
_____ 13) Junior Women's Club
_____ 14) Kiwanas
_____ 15) Knights of Columbus
_____ 16) Lions
_____ 17) Masonic Temple
_____ 18) Mocha Temple
_____ 19) Moose Club
_____ 20) recreation and park department
_____ 21) Shriners
_____ 22) sport team (Describe: _____)
_____ 23) special interest group (Describe: _____)
_____ 24) union (e.g., Teamsters, AFL-CIO)
_____ 25) United Way
_____ 26) volunteer work (Describe: _____)
_____ 27) YMCA/YWCA
_____ 28) none/don't know
_____ 29) other (Describe: _____)

b. Are there any individuals who belong to the above clubs or organizations that you wouldn't mind us contacting?

NAME	RELATIONSHIP	PHONE #	ORGANIZATION

III. Potential Support Options/Support Needs

16. Who do you live with? (check all that apply)

    _____ 1) no one

    _____ 2) parents

    _____ 3) girlfriend/boyfriend/spouse

    _____ 4) brothers/sisters

    _____ 5) relatives

    _____ 6) friends

    _____ 7) roommates

    _____ 8) personal assistant

    _____ 9) professionals/paid staff

    _____ 10) residents

    _____ 11) other (Describe: _____)

17. Who usually assists you when you need something or have a problem? (check all that apply)

    _____ 1) parent/guardian

    _____ 2) brothers/sisters

    _____ 3) girlfriend/boyfriend/spouse

    _____ 4) relatives

    _____ 5) friends

    _____ 6) community members

    _____ 7) neighbors

    _____ 8) teacher

    _____ 9) rehabilitation counselor

    _____ 10) case manager

    _____ 11) no one

    _____ 12) other (Describe: _____)

18. When you want to go somewhere, how do you usually get there? (check all that apply)

    _____ 1) drive

    _____ 2) friend or family member transports

    _____ 3) walk

    _____ 4) ride a bicycle

    _____ 5) ride the bus

    _____ 6) use a taxi

    _____ 7) use specialized transportation

    _____ 8) other (Describe: _____)

19. a. Do you receive Social Security benefits (e.g., SSI, SSDI)?

    _____ 1) yes

    _____ 2) no

(continues)

b. If yes, is the potential loss of Social Security benefits due to future employment a concern?

_____ 1) yes

_____ 2) no

20. a. Are there any types of services or supports that you would like or are in need of and are not receiving?

_____ 1) yes

_____ 2) no

b. If yes, identify the type of assistance you would like.

_____

_____

_____

_____

_____

_____

_____

_____

_____

_____

_____

_____

_____

_____

_____

_____

_____

_____

_____

_____

_____

_____

Source: *Individual Supports Assessment,* by the Rehabilitation Research and Training Center on Supported Employment, 1994, Richmond, VA: Rehabilitation Research and Training Center on Supported Employment, Virginia Commonwealth University, Natural Supports Transition Project. Copyright 1994 by the Rehabilitation Research and Training Center on Supported Employment. Reprinted with permission.

Job Site _____   Re: Participant _____

Respondent _____

Interviewer _____

Date _____

The
Environmental Job
Assessment Measure:
E-JAM

(continues)

Directions

Step 1: For each environmental cluster, have the respondent rate each descriptor and mark on the rating scale as indicated.

> **For example:**
>
> **Sit**—What percentage of the time must the participant sit on the job?
>
> **Identify and Set Goals**—How critical for success is the ability to identify and set goals on the job? If needed, use comment area for additional notes.

Step 2: Note probability of possible **Accommodations/Modifications** in the environment for each descriptor. If needed, use comment area for additional notes.

Step 3: Note possible environmental **Supports.** If needed, use comment area for additional notes.

Demands of the Job (Environmental Clusters)

General Work Behaviors (Attitudes)   **Accommodations/Modifications**   **Supports (People)**

Behavior	Rating Scale				Accommodations/Modifications					Supports
1. Attendance	Not critical	Mildly critical	Somewhat critical	Critical	NA	Low prob.	2	3	High prob.	
2. Punctuality	Not critical	Mildly critical	Somewhat critical	Critical	NA	Low prob.	2	3	High prob.	
3. Grooming/hygiene	Not critical	Mildly critical	Somewhat critical	Critical	NA	Low prob.	2	3	High prob.	
4. Attends to task (concentration)	Not critical	Mildly critical	Somewhat critical	Critical	NA	Low prob.	2	3	High prob.	
5. Work pace	Slow	2	3	Fast	NA	Low prob.	2	3	High prob.	
6. Organization	Repetitive	2	3	Varied	NA	Low prob.	2	3	High prob.	
7. Works independently	Requires supervision	2	3	Independent	NA	Low prob.	2	3	High prob.	
8. Follows directions	Simple—1,2 sequential steps	1–2 step random	3+ step sequential	3+ step random	NA	Low prob.	2	3	High prob.	
9. Flexibility (changes in job routine)	Not critical	Mildly critical	Somewhat critical	Critical	NA	Low prob.	2	3	High prob.	
10. Adheres to rules and safety regulations	Not critical	Mildly critical	Somewhat critical	Critical	NA	Low prob.	2	3	High prob.	
11. Self-aware; monitors errors	Not critical	Mildly critical	Somewhat critical	Critical	NA	Low prob.	2	3	High prob.	
12. Identifies and sets goals	Not critical	Mildly critical	Somewhat critical	Critical	NA	Low prob.	2	3	High prob.	
13. Information retrieval and use (thinks on feet)	Not critical	Mildly critical	Somewhat critical	Critical	NA	Low prob.	2	3	High prob.	
14. Prioritizes tasks	Not critical	Mildly critical	Somewhat critical	Critical	NA	Low prob.	2	3	High prob.	

Comments

Physical Demands of the Job

Accommodations/Modifications   Supports (People)

Item										Supports (People)
1. Sitting (% of job time)	25% or less	50%	75%	100%	NA	Low prob.	2	3	High prob.	
2. Standing/walking (% of job time)	25% or less	50%	75%	100%	NA	Low prob.	2	3	High prob.	
3. Strength	NA	Light	Medium	Heavy	NA	Low prob.	2	3	High prob.	
4. Eye–hand coordination/ manual dexterity	Not critical	Mildly critical	Somewhat critical	Critical	NA	Low prob.	2	3	High prob.	
5. Vision	Not critical	Mildly critical	Somewhat critical	Critical	NA	Low prob.	2	3	High prob.	
6. Hearing	Not critical	Mildly critical	Somewhat critical	Critical	NA	Low prob.	2	3	High prob.	
7. Work hours	1–2 hrs.	3–4 hrs.	5–6 hrs.	7–8 hrs.	NA	Low prob.	2	3	High prob.	

Comments

Working Conditions (Physical)

Accommodations/Modifications   Supports (People)

Item										Supports (People)
1. Inside	25% or less	50%	75%	100%	NA	Low prob.	2	3	High prob.	
2. Variation in environmental temperature	Not characteristic of the job	Mildly	Somewhat	Very characteristic	NA	Low prob.	2	3	High prob.	
3. Presence of fumes, dust, odor in the air	Not characteristic of the job	Mildly	Somewhat	Very characteristic	NA	Low prob.	2	3	High prob.	
4. Mechanical hazards	Not characteristic of the job	Mildly	Somewhat	Very characteristic	NA	Low prob.	2	3	High prob.	
5. Noise	Not characteristic of the job	Mildly	Somewhat	Very characteristic	NA	Low prob.	2	3	High prob.	
6. Wet/damp	Not characteristic of the job	Mildly	Somewhat	Very characteristic	NA	Low prob.	2	3	High prob.	
7. Presence of dirt in environment	Not characteristic of the job	Mildly	Somewhat	Very characteristic	NA	Low prob.	2	3	High prob.	
8. Varied lighting	Not characteristic of the job	Mildly	Somewhat	Very characteristic	NA	Low prob.	2	3	High prob.	
9. Frequent changes/multiple placements on the job	Not characteristic of the job	Mildly	Somewhat	Very characteristic	NA	Low prob.	2	3	High prob.	

Comments

(continues)

Educational Demands   Accommodations/Modifications   Supports (People)

Educational Demands										Accommodations/Modifications	Supports (People)
1. Educational requirements	None	High School (GED)	Some course-work	Some com. college or more	NA	Low prob.	2	3	High prob.		
2. Specialized job-related vocabulary	Not critical	Mildly critical	Somewhat critical	Very critical	NA	Low prob.	2	3	High prob.		
3. Reading comprehension	Words/ sentences	Short sentences	Advanced inference	Abstract	NA	Low prob.	2	3	High prob.		
4. Writing	Functional fill out forms	Basic paragraph	Advanced	Abstract	NA	Low prob.	2	3	High prob.		
5. Math computation	Functional basic comp. ($\pm, \times, \div$)	Basic (fractions, decimals, %)	Advanced (algebra/ geometry)	Abstract (calculus) or more	NA	Low prob.	2	3	High prob.		
6. Attention to visual detail	Not critical	Mildly critical	Somewhat critical	Very critical	NA	Low prob.	2	3	High prob.		
7. Oral communication— receptive (listening, remembering, understanding)	Not critical	Mildly critical	Somewhat critical	Very critical	NA	Low prob.	2	3	High prob.		
8. Oral communication— expressive (speaking)	Not critical	Mildly critical	Somewhat critical	Very critical	NA	Low prob.	2	3	High prob.		
9. Problem solving	Not critical	Mildly critical	Somewhat critical	Very critical	NA	Low prob.	2	3	High prob.		
10. Computer skills	Not critical	Mildly critical	Somewhat critical	Very critical	NA	Low prob.	2	3	High prob.		
11. Use of specialized equipment	Not critical	Mildly critical	Somewhat critical	Very critical	NA	Low prob.	2	3	High prob.		
Comments											

Social Interaction on the Job   Accommodations/Modifications   Supports (People)

Social Interaction on the Job										Accommodations/Modifications	Supports (People)
1. Interacts with others (coworkers, customers)	Not critical	Mildly critical	Somewhat critical	Critical	NA	Low prob.	2	3	High prob.		
2. Interacts with supervisors	Not critical	Mildly critical	Somewhat critical	Critical	NA	Low prob.	2	3	High prob.		
3. Asks for assistance	Not critical	Mildly critical	Somewhat critical	Critical	NA	Low prob.	2	3	High prob.		
4. Accepts and uses feedback	Not critical	Mildly critical	Somewhat critical	Critical	NA	Low prob.	2	3	High prob.		
5. Group work/team work	Not critical	Mildly critical	Somewhat critical	Critical	NA	Low prob.	2	3	High prob.		
6. Takes supervision from more than one supervisor/ coworker	Not critical	Mildly critical	Somewhat critical	Critical	NA	Low prob.	2	3	High prob.		
Comments											

Source: "Environmental Assessment," by M. Waintrup and P. Kelley, in *Functional Assessment in Transition and Rehabilitation for Adolescents and Adults with Learning Disabilities* (pp. 59–62), by M. Bullis and C. Davis (Eds.), 1999, Austin, TX: PRO-ED. Copyright 1999 by PRO-ED, Inc. Reprinted with permission.

Name: _____ Date: _____

Sample Student Interview Form

DIRECTIONS: Interview the student and record responses.

A. ATTITUDE TOWARD DISABILITY

1. Tell me about your disability.

2. Are you in a special education program? Which one? Why?

3. How do you feel about this program? Is it helpful?

B. INTERESTS IN LEISURE ACTIVITIES

1. What do you do in your spare time? Sports? Hobbies? Church? Extracurricular clubs at school?

2. What chores do you do at home?

3. Do you have friends? What do you and your friends do together?

4. On a perfect Saturday, what would you do?

C. FAMILY RELATIONSHIPS

1. What do you like best about your family?

2. Who usually helps you with schoolwork or other problems?

3. Is there anything that causes difficulties for you at home?

D. FUNCTIONAL SKILLS

1. If you had a job, how would you get to work?

2. Who selects your clothes?

3. Do you shop alone for your personal things?

4. Do you have an allowance or personal money from a job?

5. If you were home alone at dinner time, what would you eat and what would you do to prepare this meal?

6. If you had $1000, what would you buy?

E. EDUCATIONAL INTERESTS

1. What classes would you like to take? Would you like to include vocational classes?

2. Of all the classes you have taken, which one was the best? Why?

3. Do you want to go to school after high school? Where?

4. What do your parents want you to do after high school?

(continues)

F. WORK AND CLASS PREFERENCES

1. What teachers do you like best? Why?

    Least? Why?

2. Do you like to work alone or in a group?

3. When you work, do you like to sit most of the time or move around?

4. Do you prefer to work inside or outside?

5. Do you like to work on a computer?

6. Do you like to help people? Or work with things?

G. OCCUPATIONAL AND CAREER AWARENESS

1. Name as many jobs as you can. (time limit: 2 minutes)

2. Where do you begin to find a job?

3. What are some reasons people get fired?

4. What should you do when you are going to be absent or late to work?

H. FUTURE PLANS

1. What will you be doing during the next year, in 5 years, in 10 years toward the following postschool outcomes?

    Employment:

    Education:

    Living arrangements:

2. Will you need help meeting your goals? Which one(s)?

3. Where would you get the help you need?

4. What concerns you most about the future?

Source: "Preparing Students for Transition," by C. Dowdy and R. Evers, 1996, *Intervention in School and Clinic, 31*(4), p. 203. Copyright 1996 by PRO-ED, Inc. Reprinted with permission.

Further Education/Training

Study Skills Inventory

Completed by: _____ Student: _____ Date: _____

Place the appropriate number (1, 2, or 3) in the box next to each study skill subskill (1 = Mastered—regular, appropriate use of skill; 2 = Partially Mastered—needs some improvement; 3 = Not Mastered—infrequent use of skill).

Reading Rate

☐ Skimming
☐ Scanning
☐ Rapid reading
☐ Normal rate
☐ Study or careful reading
☐ Understands importance of reading rates

Listening

☐ Attends to listening activities
☐ Applies meaning to verbal messages
☐ Filters out auditory distractions
☐ Comprehends verbal messages
☐ Understands importance of listening skills

Note Taking/Outlining

☐ Uses headings/subheadings appropriately
☐ Takes brief and clear notes
☐ Records essential information
☐ Applies skill during writing activities
☐ Uses skill during lectures

☐ Develops organized outlines
☐ Follows consistent notetaking format
☐ Understands importance of note taking
☐ Understands importance of outlining

Report Writing

☐ Organizes thoughts in writing
☐ Completes written reports from outline
☐ Includes only necessary information
☐ Uses proper sentence structure
☐ Uses proper punctuation
☐ Uses proper grammar and spelling
☐ Proofreads written assignments
☐ States clear introductory statement
☐ Includes clear concluding statements
☐ Understands importance of writing reports

Oral Presentations

☐ Freely participates in oral presentations

☐ Oral presentations are well organized

☐ Uses gestures appropriately

☐ Speaks clearly

☐ Uses proper language when reporting orally

☐ Understands importance of oral reporting

Graphic Aids

☐ Attends to relevant elements in visual material

☐ Uses visuals appropriately in presentations

☐ Develops own graphic material

☐ Is not confused or distracted by visual material in presentations

☐ Understands importance of visual material

Test Taking

☐ Studies for tests in an organized way

☐ Spends appropriate amount of time studying different topics covered on a test

☐ Avoids cramming for tests

☐ Organizes narrative responses appropriately

☐ Reads and understands directions before answering questions

☐ Proofreads responses and checks for errors

☐ Identifies and uses clue words in questions

☐ Properly records answers

☐ Saves difficult items until last

☐ Eliminates obvious wrong answers

☐ Systematically reviews completed tests to determine test-taking or test-studying errors

☐ Corrects previous test-taking errors

☐ Understands importance of test-taking skills

Library Usage

☐ Uses cataloging system (card or computerized) effectively

☐ Able to locate library materials

☐ Understands organizational layout of library

☐ Understands and uses services of media specialist

☐ Understands overall functions and purposes of a library

☐ Understands importance of library usage skills

Reference Materials

☐ Able to identify components of different reference materials

☐ Uses guide words appropriately

☐ Consults reference materials when necessary

☐ Uses materials appropriately to complete assignments

(*continues*)

Study Skills Inventory (continued)

☐ Able to identify different types of reference materials and sources
☐ Understands importance of reference materials

Time Management

☐ Completes tasks on time
☐ Plans and organizes daily activities and responsibilities effectively
☐ Plans and organizes weekly and monthly schedules
☐ Reorganizes priorities when necessary
☐ Meets scheduled deadlines
☐ Accurately perceives the amount of time required to complete tasks

☐ Adjusts time allotment to complete tasks
☐ Accepts responsibility for managing own time
☐ Understands importance of effective time management

Self-Management

☐ Monitors own behavior
☐ Changes own behavior as necessary
☐ Thinks before acting
☐ Responsible for own behavior
☐ Identifies behaviors that interfere with own learning
☐ Understands importance of self-management

Summary of Study Skill Proficiency

Summarize in the chart below the number of Mastered (1), Partially Mastered (2), and Not Mastered (3) study skill subskills. The number next to each study skill represents the total number of subskills for each area.

Study Skill	M	PM	NM	Study Skill	M	PM	NM
Reading Rate–6				Test Taking–13			
Listening–5				Library Usage–6			
Notetaking/Outlining–9				Reference Materials–6			
Report Writing–10				Time Management–9			
Oral Presentations–6				Self-Management–6			
Graphic Aids–5							

Summary Comments:

Source: Teaching Students with Learning Problems To Use Study Skills: A Teacher's Guide, by J. Hoover and J. Patton, 1995, Austin, TX: PRO-ED. Copyright 1995 by PRO-ED, Inc. Reprinted with permission.

World Wide Web
Self-Assessment Skill Checklist

Name: _____ Date: _____

Type of Computer (circle one): IBM/compatible Macintosh

Type of Browser (circle one): America Online Microsoft Internet Explorer Netscape Navigator

Check your skill level prior to this course in the Pre column. At the conclusion of the course, check your skill level in the Post column.

	Pre	Post
AWARENESS		
I have heard of the World Wide Web (WWW).	_____	_____
I know someone who has surfed the Web.	_____	_____
I have used a web browser to surf the Web.	_____	_____
I know where/how I could access the Web at home or work.	_____	_____
BASIC SKILLS		
Demonstrate the ability to point and click.	_____	_____
Locate Netscape (or other browser) on the computer hard drive and initiate the program.	_____	_____
Recognize a home page.	_____	_____
Enter a WWW address into Netscape (or other browser).	_____	_____
Demonstrate the ability to use scroll bars.	_____	_____
Recognize the visual cues indicating a link.	_____	_____
Demonstrate the ability to select and access a link.	_____	_____
Demonstrate the ability to use the "Back" button.	_____	_____
INTERMEDIATE SKILLS		
Demonstrate the ability to conduct a search on the Web.	_____	_____
Obtain "copies" of selected information using the options for (a) Save As, (b) Mail Document, and (c) Print.	_____	_____
Collect addresses of useful Web sites.	_____	_____
ADVANCED SKILLS		
Feel comfortable in teaching others how to navigate the Web.	_____	_____
Demonstrate the ability to create a home page.	_____	_____
Demonstrate the ability to create working links.	_____	_____
Demonstrate the ability to copy selected portions of html code from a page and insert this code into a personal home page (i.e., graphic, animation, format, etc.).	_____	_____

Source: "Self-Assessment Skill Checklist," by D. L. Edyburn, May/June 1998, *Teaching Exceptional Children,* p. 7. Copyright 1998 by the Council for Exceptional Children. Reprinted with permission.

What To Consider When Exploring Military Training

Think about these questions before, during, and after an appointment with a military recruiter.

1. What is the minimum tour of duty (time commitment)?

2. What kind of training will they give me in my interest area(s)? How can I apply it to civilian life?

3. How will my learning disability affect my ability to fulfill expectations in the military? Will there be ways to accommodate problem areas?

4. Where might I be stationed?

5. Is the military consistent with my career interests, aptitudes, and values?

6. How do military training and work opportunities compare with civilian training and work opportunities I might have?

Source: Tools for Transition: Student Handbook, by E. P. Aune and J. E. Ness, 1991, Circle Pines, MN: American Guidance Service. Copyright 1991 by American Guidance Service. Reprinted with permission.

Postsecondary Course Analysis Guide

Course Number/Title: ______________________ Instructor: ______________________

A. Course Materials

1. Which of these materials are used in this course?

	Degree of Usage				
	Never				Constant
_____ required texts	1	2	3	4	5
_____ optional texts	1	2	3	4	5
_____ reserve readings	1	2	3	4	5
_____ handouts	1	2	3	4	5
_____ Internet resources	1	2	3	4	5
_____ other (specify): ______________________	1	2	3	4	5

B. Content Presentation

1. Which format is used in class sessions?

	Relative Frequency				
	Never				Always
_____ lecture	1	2	3	4	5
_____ class discussion	1	2	3	4	5
_____ small group activities	1	2	3	4	5
_____ specific in-class assignments (e.g., writing assignments)	1	2	3	4	5
_____ student presentation/performance	1	2	3	4	5
_____ other (specify): ______________________	1	2	3	4	5

2. Which instructional techniques are used in the course?

	Degree of Usage				
	Never				Constant
_____ handouts	1	2	3	4	5
_____ advance organizers (lecture outlines)	1	2	3	4	5
_____ computer-based presentations	1	2	3	4	5
_____ overhead projector	1	2	3	4	5
_____ other audiovisual aids specify: ______________________	1	2	3	4	5
_____ blackboard	1	2	3	4	5
_____ Internet-based activities	1	2	3	4	5
_____ field-based experience	1	2	3	4	5
_____ other (specify): ______________________	1	2	3	4	5

3. Are there personal idiosyncracies of the instructor(s) that may positively and/or negatively affect students' success in the course? ______________________

____

C. Student Responsibilities

1. Which of the following tasks are students required to perform *in class?*

	Relative Frequency				
	Never				Always
_____ note taking from lectures/presentations	1	2	3	4	5
_____ respond to direct questioning	1	2	3	4	5
_____ reading assignments	1	2	3	4	5
_____ writing assignments	1	2	3	4	5
_____ independent work activities	1	2	3	4	5
_____ small group work/discussion	1	2	3	4	5
_____ class participation	1	2	3	4	5
_____ class oral presentation	1	2	3	4	5
_____ other (specify): ______________________	1	2	3	4	5

(*continues*)

2. Which tasks are students required to perform *out of class*?

	Relative Frequency				
	Never				Always
	1	2	3	4	5
_____ reading assignments	1	2	3	4	5
_____ writing assignments	1	2	3	4	5
_____ Internet-based activities	1	2	3	4	5
_____ short papers	1	2	3	4	5
_____ term papers	1	2	3	4	5
_____ field work	1	2	3	4	5
_____ course projects	1	2	3	4	5
_____ interviews	1	2	3	4	5
_____ extra credit (options available)	1	2	3	4	5
_____ other (specify): _____	1	2	3	4	5

D. Student Evaluation

1. How are students evaluated in this course?

	Degree of Usage				
	Never				Constant
_____ tests	1	2	3	4	5
_____ papers	1	2	3	4	5
_____ performance measures	1	2	3	4	5
_____ in-class presentations	1	2	3	4	5
_____ projects (group)	1	2	3	4	5
_____ projects (individual)	1	2	3	4	5
_____ field work	1	2	3	4	5
_____ other (specify): _____	1	2	3	4	5

2. What types of tests and/or test items are used in this course?

	Degree of Usage				
	Never				Always
_____ no testing is done	1	2	3	4	5
_____ essay	1	2	3	4	5
_____ multiple choice	1	2	3	4	5
_____ other objective tests (i.e., matching, T/F)	1	2	3	4	5
_____ completion/short answer	1	2	3	4	5
_____ oral exams	1	2	3	4	5
_____ performance of skill	1	2	3	4	5
_____ other (specify): _____	1	2	3	4	5

E. Classroom Standards

1. What standards apply in this class? Are they stated or implied? Specify.

_____ attendance: _____

_____ lateness: _____

_____ attentiveness during class: _____

_____ preparation _____

    _____ coursework (e.g., reading assignments): _____

    _____ materials for class: _____

_____ grade of incomplete: _____

_____ other (specify): _____

_____

2. How is feedback given to students?

_____ grades only

_____ corrective feedback (i.e., comments)

_____ primary focus on errors

_____ other (specify): _____

_____

3. Are there other special requirements that contribute to student evaluation (e.g., typing of papers, late acceptance)? _____

4. Are there stipulations that interfere with the use of tape recorders (Y/N), interpreters (Y/N), notetakers (Y/N)? _____

F. Student Supports

1. Which of the following course-related support systems are available?

	Degree of Availability				
	Nonexistent			Very Available	
_____ accommodation of student needs	1	2	3	4	5
_____ instructor access	1	2	3	4	5
_____ teaching assistant(s) access	1	2	3	4	5
_____ course mailing list (i.e., listserve)	1	2	3	4	5
_____ Web-based resources	1	2	3	4	5
_____ special study sessions	1	2	3	4	5
_____ peer support mechanisms	1	2	3	4	5
_____ other (specify): _____	1	2	3	4	5

Source: "Analyzing College Courses," by J. R. Patton and E. A. Polloway, 1987, *Academic Therapy, 22,* pp. 273–280. Copyright 1987 by PRO-ED, Inc. Adapted with permission.

School/Program _____   Re: Participant _____

Respondent _____

Interviewer _____

Date _____

The
Environmental School
Assessment Measure:
E-SAM

Directions

Step 1: For each environmental cluster, have the respondent rate each descriptor and mark on the rating scale as indicated.

For example:

Hearing—How critical is the ability to hear well to success in the school setting?

Reading Comprehension—What level of reading comprehension is required for success in the school setting?

If needed, use comment area for additional notes.

Step 2: Note probability of possible **Accommodations/Modifications** in the environment for each descriptor. If needed, use comment area for additional notes.

Step 3: Note possible environmental **Supports.** If needed, use comment area for additional notes.

Demands of the School (Environmental Clusters)

Physical Demands					Accommodations/Modifications					Supports (People)
1. Sitting (% of school time)	25% or less	50%	75%	100%	NA	Low prob.	2	3	High prob.	
2. Standing/walking (% of school time)	25% or less	50%	75%	100%	NA	Low prob.	2	3	High prob.	
3. Strength	NA	Light	Medium	Heavy	NA	Low prob.	2	3	High prob.	
4. Eye–hand coordination/ manual dexterity	Not critical	Mildly critical	Somewhat critical	Critical	NA	Low prob.	2	3	High prob.	
5. Vision	Not critical	Mildly critical	Somewhat critical	Critical	NA	Low prob.	2	3	High prob.	
6. Hearing	Not critical	Mildly critical	Somewhat critical	Critical	NA	Low prob.	2	3	High prob.	
7. Number of daily class hours	1–2 hrs.	3–4 hrs.	5–6 hrs.	7–8 hrs.	NA	Low prob.	2	3	High prob.	
8. Inside	25% or less	50%	75%	100%	NA	Low prob.	2	3	High prob.	
9. Varied environmental temperature	Not characteristic	Mildly	Somewhat	Very characteristic	NA	Low prob.	2	3	High prob.	
10. Presence of fumes, dust, odor in the air	Not characteristic	Mildly	Somewhat	Very characteristic	NA	Low prob.	2	3	High prob.	
11. Mechanical hazards	Not characteristic	Mildly	Somewhat	Very characteristic	NA	Low prob.	2	3	High prob.	
12. Noise	Not characteristic	Mildly	Somewhat	Very characteristic	NA	Low prob.	2	3	High prob.	
13. Wet/damp	Not characteristic	Mildly	Somewhat	Very characteristic	NA	Low prob.	2	3	High prob.	
14. Presence of dirt in environment	Not characteristic	Mildly	Somewhat	Very characteristic	NA	Low prob.	2	3	High prob.	
15. Varied lighting	Not characteristic	Mildly	Somewhat	Very characteristic	NA	Low prob.	2	3	High prob.	
Comments										

(continues)

Educational Requirements　　　　　　　　　　　　　　　　　　　　　　**Accommodations/Modifications**　　**Supports (People)**

Educational Requirements	None	High School (GED)	Some com. college	Some com. college or more	NA	Low prob.	2	3	High prob.	Supports (People)
1. Program entry requirements	None	High School (GED)	Some com. college	Some com. college or more	NA	Low prob.	2	3	High prob.	
2. Program completion requirements	Attendance	Test	Credit hours	Credit hours plus tests	NA	Low prob.	2	3	High prob.	
3. Concentration	Not critical	Mildly critical	Somewhat critical	Critical	NA	Low prob.	2	3	High prob.	
4. Work pace	Slow	2	3	Fast	NA	Low prob.	2	3	High prob.	
5. Works independently	Requires supervision	2	3	Independent actions	NA	Low prob.	2	3	High prob.	
6. Follows oral directions	Not critical	Mildly critical	Somewhat critical	Critical	NA	Low prob.	2	3	High prob.	
7. Self-aware; monitors errors	Not critical	Mildly critical	Somewhat critical	Critical	NA	Low prob.	2	3	High prob.	
8. Reading comprehension (includes following written directions)	Functional K–6	Basic 7–9	Advanced 10–12	Abstract 12+	NA	Low prob.	2	3	High prob.	
9. Writing	Functional K–6	Basic 7–9	Advanced 10–12	Abstract 12+	NA	Low prob.	2	3	High prob.	
10. Math computation	Functional K–6	Basic 7–9	Advanced 10–12	Abstract 12+	NA	Low prob.	2	3	High prob.	
11. Attends to visual detail	Not critical	Mildly critical	Somewhat critical	Very critical	NA	Low prob.	2	3	High prob.	
12. Oral communication– receptive (listening, remembering, understanding)	Functional K–6	Basic 7–9	Advanced 10–12	Abstract 12+	NA	Low prob.	2	3	High prob.	
13. Oral communication– expressive (listening)	Functional K–6	Basic 7–9	Advanced 10–12	Abstract 12+	NA	Low prob.	2	3	High prob.	
14. Problem solving	Not critical	Mildly critical	Somewhat critical	Very critical	NA	Low prob.	2	3	High prob.	
15. Computer skills	Not critical	Mildly critical	Somewhat critical	Very critical	NA	Low prob.	2	3	High prob.	
16. Task completion/follow through	Not critical	Mildly critical	Somewhat critical	Very critical	NA	Low prob.	2	3	High prob.	

Comments

General Socioeducational Expectations   **Accommodations/Modifications**   **Supports (People)**

1. Attendance	Not critical	Mildly critical	Somewhat critical	Critical	NA	Low prob.	2	3	High prob.	
2. Punctuality	Not critical	Mildly critical	Somewhat critical	Critical	NA	Low prob.	2	3	High prob.	
3. Grooming/hygiene	Not critical	Mildly critical	Somewhat critical	Critical	NA	Low prob.	2	3	High prob.	
4. Flexibility (changes in routine)	Not critical	Mildly critical	Somewhat critical	Critical	NA	Low prob.	2	3	High prob.	
5. Adheres to rules	Not critical	Mildly critical	Somewhat critical	Critical	NA	Low prob.	2	3	High prob.	
6. Interacts with peers	Not critical	Mildly critical	Somewhat critical	Critical	NA	Low prob.	2	3	High prob.	
7. Interacts with instructors	Not critical	Mildly critical	Somewhat critical	Critical	NA	Low prob.	2	3	High prob.	
8. Asks for assistance	Not critical	Mildly critical	Somewhat critical	Critical	NA	Low prob.	2	3	High prob.	
9. Accepts and uses feedback	Not critical	Mildly critical	Somewhat critical	Critical	NA	Low prob.	2	3	High prob.	
10. Time management	Not critical	Mildly critical	Somewhat critical	Critical	NA	Low prob.	2	3	High prob.	
11. Identifies and sets goals	Not critical	Mildly critical	Somewhat critical	Critical	NA	Low prob.	2	3	High prob.	
Comments										

Instructional Style/Evaluation/Materials   **Accommodations/Modifications**   **Supports (People)**

1. Teaching style—oral	25% or less	50%	75%	100%	NA	Low prob.	2	3	High prob.	
2. Teaching style—visual	25% or less	50%	75%	100%	NA	Low prob.	2	3	High prob.	
3. Teaching style—hands-on	25% or less	50%	75%	100%	NA	Low prob.	2	3	High prob.	
4. Evaluation—written	25% or less	50%	75%	100%	NA	Low prob.	2	3	High prob.	
5. Evaluation—oral	25% or less	50%	75%	100%	NA	Low prob.	2	3	High prob.	
6. Evaluation—demonstration/ projects	25% or less	50%	75%	100%	NA	Low prob.	2	3	High prob.	
7. Materials—visual (pictures, graphs, etc.)	25% or less	50%	75%	100%	NA	Low prob.	2	3	High prob.	
8. Materials—auditory	25% or less	50%	75%	100%	NA	Low prob.	2	3	High prob.	
9. Materials—written	25% or less	50%	75%	100%	NA	Low prob.	2	3	High prob.	
10. Computer use	25% or less	50%	75%	100%	NA	Low prob.	2	3	High prob.	
11. Other equipment use	25% or less	50%	75%	100%	NA	Low prob.	2	3	High prob.	
Comments										

Source: "Environmental Assessment," by M. Waintrup and P. Kelley, in *Functional Assessment in Transition and Rehabilitation for Adolescents and Adults with Learning Disabilities* (pp. 59–62), by M. Bullis and C. Davis (Eds.), 1999, Austin, TX: PRO-ED. Copyright 1999 by PRO-ED, Inc. Reprinted with permission.

Name: _____ Date: _____

Things That Are Difficult for Me

Characteristic	Yes	No	Sometimes
I have a hard time paying attention in class.			
I'm easily distracted by noises and movements.			
It's difficult for me to memorize information.			
I forget what I'm supposed to do after instruction.			
I have trouble figuring out new words.			
I have difficulty understanding what I read.			
Reading out loud is embarrassing for me.			
I can spell words, but then forget them.			
My handwriting is hard to read.			
I have trouble writing sentences and paragraphs.			
I forget how to do math calculation problems.			
Math word problems are hard for me.			
My memory for math facts is poor.			
I forget materials I need for class.			
I lose track of time and don't finish tasks.			
I misunderstand what people say to me.			
I miss important information when I listen.			
I have a hard time saying what I mean.			
I am easily frustrated and lack confidence.			
Making friends is hard for me.			

Source: Holding the Road: Student Self-Advocacy, by T. Long, B. Austin, and J. Bowen, 1998, Atlanta, GA: L.A.B. Educational Press. Copyright 1998 by L.A.B. Educational Press. Reprinted with permission.

Daily Living

Independent Living Assessment Instrument

I. Independent Living Assessment (Verbal)

Goal: *To discriminate ability for safe independent living within an apartment setting*

A. Hygiene, personal cleanliness, and clothing

   1. How did you dress today?

   2. Did the weather outside influence your choice of clothes?

   3. Do you like to take a bath or a shower?

   4. Can you describe your routine for bathing or showering and dressing to me?

   5. How do you shop for clothes? Do you like to go by yourself or with a friend?

   6. When is it important to wash your hands?

   7. How often do you brush your teeth?

   8. How often do you wash your hair?

   9. How do you handle hygiene when you have your period?

B. Apartment cleanliness and care

   1. Do you do all of your own housekeeping? If you need help with it, who do you ask and how?

   2. What would you do if your toilet backed up onto the bathroom floor?

   3. Where is the garbage kept?

   4. What would you do if you saw bugs in your apartment?

   5. Who would you call if:

      a. The sink was clogged?

      b. Something was broken?

      c. The heat was not working?

   6. Do you have a special day to do your laundry? Do you do it with assistance or independently?

C. Kitchen skills

   1. What are your favorite meals to cook?

   2. Tell me about the word *nutrition*.

   3. Do you shop for food on your own or with another person?

   4. Can you show me where you keep:

      a. TV dinners?

      b. Hamburger, other meats?

      c. Cheese?

      d. Unopened cans of fruit?

      e. Open cans of food?

      f. Milk?

      g. Cereal?

5. What happens to food when the refrigerator breaks?

6. How can you tell if food is spoiled?

7. Can you show me how you:
   a. Wash dishes?
   b. Broil a steak?
   c. Bake a chicken?
   d. Boil eggs; water?
   e. Clean floor?
   f. Store paper products?
   g. Clean refrigerator?

D. Body care, first aid, emergencies, and safety

   1. What happens when you are sick?

   2. What would you do if you cut your finger and it was bleeding?

   3. When might you need to call the emergency number?

   4. When do you stay home from work because you are not feeling well?

   5. Do you have a doctor whom you see when you are not feeling well? When have you needed to call him or her?

   6. If someone has a seizure, what could you do?

   7. What would you do if you smelled smoke or suspected a fire?

   8. If there were a fire in your building, what would you do?

   9. Are there precautions you can take to avoid having a fire occur in your apartment?

   10. When someone knocks at your door, do you open it right away?

   11. If someone were breaking into your apartment, what would you do?

   12. When someone buzzes your apartment, do you check to see who it is before allowing them to enter the building?

E. Use of Public Transportation, Community Resources, and Leisure Time

   1. How often do you take the metro bus?

   2. How did you learn the routes that you use?

   3. How do you find out about new activities?

   4. Do you travel alone at times? Are there times when you prefer going with a friend?

   5. How do you get to the grocery store? Is there a convenience store nearby for quick trips?

   6. How do you spend evenings home alone when nothing special is going on?

Source: A Guide to Vocational Assessment (3rd ed.), by P. W. Power, 2000, Austin, TX: PRO-ED. Copyright 2000 by PRO-ED, Inc. Reprinted with permission.

Name: _____   Date: _____

PARENTS OF TEENAGERS
SURVIVAL CHECKLIST

PREPARE COOKED MEALS

Can your teenagers:	no	some	usually	always
set a table?	☐	☐	☐	☐
fry bacon?	☐	☐	☐	☐
make toast?	☐	☐	☐	☐
fry and scramble eggs?	☐	☐	☐	☐
recognize basic food groups?	☐	☐	☐	☐
prepare a balanced diet for a day?	☐	☐	☐	☐
prepare a balanced diet for a week?	☐	☐	☐	☐
recognize if foods have spoiled?	☐	☐	☐	☐
roast a variety of meats?	☐	☐	☐	☐
mash potatoes?	☐	☐	☐	☐
make salads?	☐	☐	☐	☐
cook vegetables?	☐	☐	☐	☐

COMPARISON SHOPPING

Groceries

Can your teenagers:	no	some	usually	always
select fresh fruits and vegetables?	☐	☐	☐	☐
purchase a week's supply of food?	☐	☐	☐	☐
buy within a budget?	☐	☐	☐	☐
select quality meats?	☐	☐	☐	☐
compare prices?	☐	☐	☐	☐
compare sizes? (can they recognize that a 12 ounce package of bacon is more expensive than a one pound package that is listed at the same price?)	☐	☐	☐	☐
take advantage of sale items?	☐	☐	☐	☐
use coupons?	☐	☐	☐	☐
determine what items have a long shelf-life?	☐	☐	☐	☐
identify what items spoil quickly?	☐	☐	☐	☐
make up a shopping list?	☐	☐	☐	☐

COMPARISON SHOPPING

Wearing Apparel

Can your teenagers:	no	some	usually	always
plan a wardrobe that includes school, leisure, and dress clothes?	☐	☐	☐	☐
buy shoes that fit?	☐	☐	☐	☐
recognize types of materials?	☐	☐	☐	☐
check the quality of items?	☐	☐	☐	☐
check seams to see how well they are constructed?	☐	☐	☐	☐
realize bargains?	☐	☐	☐	☐
take advantage of sales?	☐	☐	☐	☐
compare prices?	☐	☐	☐	☐
know to keep sales slips?	☐	☐	☐	☐
know how to return items?	☐	☐	☐	☐
figure percentages on sales items?	☐	☐	☐	☐

COMPARISON SHOPPING

Appliances

Can your teenagers:	no	some	usually	always
compare prices?	☐	☐	☐	☐
check for quality?	☐	☐	☐	☐
evaluate discounts?	☐	☐	☐	☐

GEOGRAPHY

Can your teenagers:	no	some	usually	always
navigate to most areas of your city?	☐	☐	☐	☐
name surrounding towns and cities?	☐	☐	☐	☐
use a road map?	☐	☐	☐	☐
tell you in which country they live?	☐	☐	☐	☐
read road signs?	☐	☐	☐	☐
ask help in directions?	☐	☐	☐	☐

MATHEMATICS

Can your teenagers:

	no	some	usually	always
add?	☐	☐	☐	☐
subtract?	☐	☐	☐	☐
multiply?	☐	☐	☐	☐
divide?	☐	☐	☐	☐
figure averages?	☐	☐	☐	☐
figure percentages?	☐	☐	☐	☐
make change for one dollar?	☐	☐	☐	☐
make change for ten dollars?	☐	☐	☐	☐
make change for one hundred dollars?	☐	☐	☐	☐
tell time?	☐	☐	☐	☐
measure in inches?	☐	☐	☐	☐
measure in feet?	☐	☐	☐	☐
measure in yards?	☐	☐	☐	☐

recognize common measurements and compare them? Such as:

	no	some	usually	always
a teaspoon?	☐	☐	☐	☐
a tablespoon?	☐	☐	☐	☐
a cup?	☐	☐	☐	☐
a pint?	☐	☐	☐	☐
a quart?	☐	☐	☐	☐
a gallon?	☐	☐	☐	☐

READING

Can your teenagers read:

	no	some	usually	always
a novel?	☐	☐	☐	☐
the daily newspaper?	☐	☐	☐	☐
directions on medicine bottles?	☐	☐	☐	☐
directions on detergent boxes?	☐	☐	☐	☐
cookbook instructions?	☐	☐	☐	☐
monthly statements?	☐	☐	☐	☐
traffic signs and symbols?	☐	☐	☐	☐
an index in a book?	☐	☐	☐	☐
and use a telephone book?	☐	☐	☐	☐
and use the white pages?	☐	☐	☐	☐
and use the yellow pages?	☐	☐	☐	☐
and use the encyclopedia?	☐	☐	☐	☐
and use a library?	☐	☐	☐	☐

HOME MAINTENANCE

Can your teenagers:

	no	some	usually	always
replace a light switch?	☐	☐	☐	☐
check the safety of an extension cord?	☐	☐	☐	☐
replace a fuse?	☐	☐	☐	☐
replace a door hinge?	☐	☐	☐	☐
replace a door knob?	☐	☐	☐	☐
hang a picture?	☐	☐	☐	☐
paint a room?	☐	☐	☐	☐
paint trim on a house?	☐	☐	☐	☐
clean out guttering?	☐	☐	☐	☐
mow the yard?	☐	☐	☐	☐
trim around walks?	☐	☐	☐	☐
use insecticides safely?	☐	☐	☐	☐
store tools?	☐	☐	☐	☐
put up a shelf?	☐	☐	☐	☐
set a thermostat?	☐	☐	☐	☐
replace and clean furnace and air-conditioner filters?	☐	☐	☐	☐
defrost a refrigerator?	☐	☐	☐	☐
clean the stove and oven?	☐	☐	☐	☐
replace light bulbs?	☐	☐	☐	☐
get a key made?	☐	☐	☐	☐
clean the house: dust, vacuum, mop, wax?	☐	☐	☐	☐
clean and disinfect a bathroom?	☐	☐	☐	☐
make a bed?	☐	☐	☐	☐
get rid of roaches?	☐	☐	☐	☐
tell which clothing should be laundered and which dry-cleaned?	☐	☐	☐	☐
wash and iron clothing?	☐	☐	☐	☐
tell which cleaning fluids are best for what jobs?	☐	☐	☐	☐
do simple mending and sew on buttons?	☐	☐	☐	☐
contact the landlord or a professional for more serious problems?	☐	☐	☐	☐

APPLIANCES

Can your teenagers operate:

	no	some	usually	always
a toaster?	☐	☐	☐	☐
a stove?	☐	☐	☐	☐
a vacuum sweeper?	☐	☐	☐	☐
a dish washer?	☐	☐	☐	☐
a clothes washer?	☐	☐	☐	☐
a clothes dryer?	☐	☐	☐	☐
a lawn mower?	☐	☐	☐	☐
a garbage disposal?	☐	☐	☐	☐
an electric mixer?	☐	☐	☐	☐
an oven?	☐	☐	☐	☐
an iron?	☐	☐	☐	☐

(continues)

CARPENTRY

Can your teenagers use a:	no	some	usually	always
hammer?	☐	☐	☐	☐
screwdriver?	☐	☐	☐	☐
pliers?	☐	☐	☐	☐
hand drill?	☐	☐	☐	☐
hand saw?	☐	☐	☐	☐
level?	☐	☐	☐	☐
square?	☐	☐	☐	☐

HEALTH

Can your teenagers:	no	some	usually	always
apply a tourniquet?	☐	☐	☐	☐
clean a cut?	☐	☐	☐	☐
apply simple bandages?	☐	☐	☐	☐
stop someone from choking on food?	☐	☐	☐	☐
give mouth to mouth resuscitation?	☐	☐	☐	☐
recognize symptoms of colds?	☐	☐	☐	☐
recognize the cause of certain pains?	☐	☐	☐	☐
treat a minor burn?	☐	☐	☐	☐
decide when to use home remedies?	☐	☐	☐	☐
decide when to go to the doctor?	☐	☐	☐	☐
administer simple medication?	☐	☐	☐	☐
identify minor infections?	☐	☐	☐	☐
use a thermometer?	☐	☐	☐	☐
supplement diet with needed vitamins?	☐	☐	☐	☐
carry out a proper program of physical exercise?	☐	☐	☐	☐

PERSONAL GROOMING

Do your teenagers:	no	some	usually	always
know how often to bathe, wash hair, brush teeth, etc.?	☐	☐	☐	☐
know the importance of using a deodorant?	☐	☐	☐	☐
know how to buy toiletries: razor blades, deodorant, toothpaste, shampoo, etc.?	☐	☐	☐	☐
recognize quality in what they buy so they won't be misled by false advertising?	☐	☐	☐	☐

	no	some	usually	always
realize the importance of making a neat, well-groomed appearance?	☐	☐	☐	☐
realize the importance of clean clothing and shined shoes?	☐	☐	☐	☐
know how to manicure their fingernails?	☐	☐	☐	☐

SEXUALITY

Do your teenagers:	no	some	usually	always
know the biological basics of sex?	☐	☐	☐	☐
understand their own sexual drives?	☐	☐	☐	☐
accept responsibility for their own sexuality?	☐	☐	☐	☐
understand birth-control measures?	☐	☐	☐	☐
understand basics of sexual hygiene?	☐	☐	☐	☐
know where to seek professional advice?	☐	☐	☐	☐
feel they can discuss problems with you?	☐	☐	☐	☐

COMMUNICATION

Can your teenagers:	no	some	usually	always
dial a long-distance number?	☐	☐	☐	☐
dial station-to-station?	☐	☐	☐	☐
dial person-to-person?	☐	☐	☐	☐
call collect?	☐	☐	☐	☐
readily find emergency numbers?	☐	☐	☐	☐
organize and compose a personal letter and thank you note?	☐	☐	☐	☐
converse well in private conversations?	☐	☐	☐	☐
state opinions backed by reason and fact?	☐	☐	☐	☐

CURRENT EVENTS

Can your teenagers:	no	some	usually	always
read the newspaper?	☐	☐	☐	☐
watch the evening news and discuss current events?	☐	☐	☐	☐
know the name of president of the United States?	☐	☐	☐	☐

TRANSPORTATION

Can your teenagers:	no	some	usually	always
use public transit systems?	☐	☐	☐	☐
drive a car safely?	☐	☐	☐	☐
recognize minor mechanical problems?	☐	☐	☐	☐
take the car to a reputable mechanic?	☐	☐	☐	☐
change a tire?	☐	☐	☐	☐
check the oil, water, transmission fluid and the windshield washer?	☐	☐	☐	☐
be responsible for seeing that the car receives proper maintenance?	☐	☐	☐	☐

EMPLOYMENT

Do your teenagers know how to:	no	some	usually	always
apply for employment?	☐	☐	☐	☐
fill out an application form?	☐	☐	☐	☐
write a business letter?	☐	☐	☐	☐
mail packages?	☐	☐	☐	☐
obtain a social security card?	☐	☐	☐	☐
use a credit card?	☐	☐	☐	☐
pay monthly bills?	☐	☐	☐	☐
balance a checkbook?	☐	☐	☐	☐
open a checking account?	☐	☐	☐	☐
keep a bank account?	☐	☐	☐	☐
open a savings account?	☐	☐	☐	☐
apply for a loan?	☐	☐	☐	☐
write checks?	☐	☐	☐	☐
fill out income tax forms?	☐	☐	☐	☐

Source: A Slice of Life, by Fremont Union High School, 1980, Sunnyvale, CA: Fremont Union School District. Copyright 1980 by Fremont Union School District. Reprinted with permission.

Assessment of Financial Skills and Abilities

Money Management and Banking

a) Budgeting

___ Knows how to save money

___ Knows how "wants" and "needs" apply to his or her life

___ Understands concept of budgeting

___ Can consider personal factors in determining a budget (e.g., important to this person to set aside money to go to dances twice a month)

___ Can compute total amount of bills owed

___ Knows how to organize receipts and bills needed to formulate a budget

___ Can resolve hypothetical budgeting problems

___ Remembers to pay bills

b) State, Federal, and Local Taxes

___ Can read words, terms, and abbreviations associated with taxes

___ Can understand the meaning of tax terminology (e.g., FICA, gross)

___ Can read own W-2 form

___ Can discuss the purpose of a W-2 form and taxes

___ Knows of the requirements for filing an income tax return

___ Knows when to file income tax

___ Able to read the IRS tax forms (e.g., 1040 EZ)

___ Knows how to identify which form to use

___ Knows how to save receipts and tax documents necessary to complete tax filing

___ Knows of tax assessor services (e.g., H & R Block)

___ Knows how to determine the cost of tax assessor services

___ Knows about various tax charges for property tax, state and federal income

c) Banking

___ Knows purpose of a checking and savings account

___ Can read and complete banking forms

___ Knows how to deposit pay or other check

___ Knows purpose of a check and responsibilities when writing a check

___ Can fill out a check completely and correctly

___ Knows how to complete check registry

___ Remembers to complete check registry

___ Can reconcile a bank statement to monitor account balance(s)

___ Can get banking questions answered by a bank representative

Comparison Shopping

___ Knows how to use unit pricing to comparison shop

___ Knows how to do computation for comparison shopping when using coupons

___ Knowledge of the concept of a sale

___ Knowledgeable of sales terminology

___ Knowledgeable about manufacturer warranties

___ Knows how to locate different types of stores and is knowledgeable about their differences (e.g., pricing, wholesale, type of merchandise sold)

___ Knows about salesperson tactics to persuade a consumer to make a purchase

Understanding Advertising

___ Can read and is familiar with terms associated with advertising
___ Knows the function of advertising
___ Can distinguish between an honest value and suspicious terms used in advertising

Credit

___ Understands concept of credit, leasing, and credit cards
___ Can complete a credit application
___ Can read credit contracts
___ Can identify the cash price and credit price of an item and calculate the difference in value
___ Knowledgeable of cash advances and different types of loans
___ Knows what to consider when borrowing money
___ Can complete a loan application
___ Knowledgeable of the different "do's" and "don'ts" of credit
___ Knowledgeable of credit rating system and the importance of a good credit rating
___ Knows consumer rights and resources pertaining to credit and loans

Purchasing and Maintaining a Car

___ Knows responsibilities of purchasing or leasing a car
___ Knowledgeable of terms associated with purchasing or leasing a car
___ Knows several places to purchase a car
___ Can read classified advertisements pertaining to car sales
___ Can distinguish factual statements from possibly misleading terminology
___ Knowledgeable of what factors to consider when purchasing a car
___ Knows the financial aspects associated with purchasing a car
___ Can determine the amount of money he or she is able to spend on the car purchase
___ Can determine the difference in the amount of money in possession and the sales price of a particular car
___ Can determine the best size, model, and so on of car that will suit his or her needs
___ Can interact with a car salesperson
___ Knowledgeable about car maintenance, its importance, and the cost of car maintenance
___ Knowledgeable of car maintenance terminology
___ Can budget for car maintenance costs
___ Knows where to take a car to get maintenance performed

Insurance

___ Knowledgeable of the concept of insurance and its purpose
___ Knowledgeable of various types of insurance (i.e., life, car, health, disability, social security, burial)
___ Knowledgeable of insurance terminology
___ Can read information describing the benefits and costs of various insurance policies
___ Knowledgeable of eligibility terms
___ Knowledgeable of what items are not covered by a given policy
___ Can compare different plans for the same type of insurance
___ Knowledgeable of social security and its benefits
___ Aware of different benefits available to persons over the age of 65
___ Knowledgeable of Medicare and who is eligible for benefits under this plan
___ Can compute how much of his or her income could be spent on insurance
___ Knows the role of an insurance agent in helping someone determine the type and amount of insurance to buy

Name: _____ Date: _____

Transportation Needs

How do you get to the places you like to go to? Do you need help finding a way to get to:

	YES	NO
Job	_____	_____
Home	_____	_____
School	_____	_____
Family	_____	_____
Friends	_____	_____

Various Community Settings:

	YES	NO
Restaurant	_____	_____
Bank	_____	_____
Grocery store	_____	_____
Laundromat	_____	_____
Post office	_____	_____
Clothing store	_____	_____
Health care facility	_____	_____
Government services	_____	_____
Social/recreational services	_____	_____
Church/synagogue/mosque	_____	_____

Other Places

_____:	_____	_____
_____:	_____	_____
_____:	_____	_____
_____:	_____	_____

Leisure Activities

Survey of Indoor and Outdoor Recreational Activities

Student's Name: _____

Today's Date: _____

Person Completing Form: _____

Directions: The student, parent/guardian, or teacher may complete this form. Place a check beside the activities that the student has participated in. For students completing this form: Circle any items that you would like to try sometime.

Indoor Activities

Structured Solo Indoor Activities

_____ Singing a requested song

_____ Reciting the alphabet/poem/story

_____ Computer games

_____ Video games

_____ Completing a puzzle

_____ Making a photo album

_____ Organizing something

_____ Listening to a talking book

_____ Reading a book/magazine/newspaper

_____ Completing a model airplane or similar project

_____ Arts and crafts

_____ Playing a specific song on a musical instrument

_____ Following a cooking recipe

_____ Sewing

_____ Taking a class for fun

_____ Other

Unstructured Solo Indoor Activities

_____ Solitary card games

_____ Make-believe play

_____ Making up songs

_____ Painting/drawing/doodling

_____ Arts and crafts

_____ Listening to music

_____ Playing a musical instrument

_____ Watching television or a movie
_____ Writing a letter
_____ Exercising indoors
_____ Applying fingernail polish/makeup
_____ Arranging flowers
_____ Giving the dog a bath
_____ Going shopping alone
_____ Playing games at an arcade
_____ Volunteering
_____ Other

Structured Team/Group Indoor Activities
_____ Board games
_____ Charades
_____ Singing together or in a choir
_____ Playing cards
_____ Following a recipe together
_____ Quilting with a group
_____ Attending a comedy club or live performance
_____ Attending a musical performance
_____ Attending an indoor sporting event
_____ Bowling
_____ Other

Unstructured Team/Group Indoor Activities
_____ Watching a movie together
_____ Eating together
_____ Dancing
_____ Socializing
_____ Socializing over the phone
_____ Visiting a museum, exhibit, or art gallery
_____ Going shopping together
_____ Other

Outdoor Activities

Structured Solo Outdoor Activities
_____ Planting a flower/tree
_____ Washing a car
_____ Yard work/mowing the yard
_____ Building a tree house or other structure
_____ Running an obstacle course
_____ Other

(continues)

113

Unstructured Solo Outdoor Activities

_____ Playing an outdoor game alone
_____ Playing with sporting equipment/toys
_____ Exercising outdoors
_____ Walking/playing with the dog
_____ Flying a kite
_____ Hiking/walking
_____ Fishing
_____ Swimming
_____ Bicycling
_____ Running
_____ Swinging
_____ Gardening
_____ Going to the park alone
_____ Making something by self outdoors
_____ Other

Structured Team/Group Outdoor Activities

_____ Exercising together
_____ Group swimming games
_____ Working on/fixing car
_____ Playing a game of baseball, golf, kickball, hide and seek, volleyball, etc.
_____ Attending an outdoor concert
_____ Christmas caroling
_____ Attending an outdoor sporting event
_____ Playing putt-putt golf
_____ Other

Unstructured Team/Group Outdoor Activities

_____ Fishing/hunting with a group
_____ Camping
_____ Bird watching
_____ Bicycling with a group
_____ Group car drive
_____ Star gazing
_____ Barbecuing
_____ Going on a picnic
_____ Attending a festival or fair
_____ Boating/sailing/canoeing or tubing
_____ Going to the park together
_____ Horseback riding

_____ Skiing or sledding
_____ Going to the zoo
_____ Visiting an amusement park
_____ Other

Questions To Consider

1. Tally up the number of checked activities for each category:

   Number of:

   _____ Structured Solo Indoor Activities   _____ Structured Solo Outdoor Activities

   _____ Unstructured Solo Indoor Activities   _____ Unstructured Solo Outdoor Activities

   _____ Structured Team/Group Indoor Activities   _____ Structured Team/Group Outdoor Activities

   _____ Unstructured Team/Group Indoor Activities   _____ Unstructured Team/Group Outdoor Activities

2. Were more indoor or outdoor activities checked off?

   Are the outdoor activities performed at the same one or two locations?

3. Were more group or solo activities checked off?

   Are the group activities performed with the same group of people?

4. Were more unstructured or structured activities checked off?

5. How many activities were selected that require a brief versus long amount of time to complete?

   Number brief: _____

   Number long: _____

6. Were more activities selected that are performed during the day or at night?

7. Are the checked-off activities age appropriate for this person?

8. Are more activities done at the school, home, or community setting?

9. Are the activities self-initiated by the student?

   Are the activities the student's choice?

   Does the student regulate how long the activity will last or how long the student will engage in the activity?

10. Are the activities constructive?

11. Does the student know how to plan for recreational activities (e.g., transportation, money, others, time)?

(continues)

12. Does the student possess adequate social skills to participate successfully in team/group activities?

13. Is the student knowledgeable of the rules or expectations of the activities he or she engages in?

14. Does the student seem to enjoy or relax during particular recreational activities?

15. Which individual interests and preferences are emerging as the strongest choices?

16. Has the student developed any lifelong interests, hobbies, or activities?

17. Did you notice any other patterns?

Name: _____ Date: _____

Recreation and Leisure Survey

PREFERENCES

1. What recreational and leisure *activities* are chosen when given freedom to choose?

   _____

   _____

   _____

2. What recreational and leisure *settings* are chosen when given freedom to choose?

   _____

   _____

   _____

FUNCTIONING AND CAPABILITY

1. What recreational and leisure skills are currently used?

   _____

   _____

   _____

2. What recreational and leisure skills are possible if given an opportunity?

   _____

   _____

   _____

3. What recreational and leisure skills are possible if given instruction?

   _____

   _____

   _____

(continues)

Recreation and Leisure Survey (Continued)

PHYSICAL CHARACTERISTICS

1. What physical characteristics exist or may be lacking that may interfere with recreational and leisure development?

_____

_____

_____

2. What physical characteristics exist that may promote recreational and leisure development?

_____

_____

_____

AGE APPROPRIATENESS

1. Are the recreational and leisure preferences age appropriate? _____

2. Are the recreational and leisure skills used age appropriate? _____

ACCESS TO RESOURCES

1. Are community recreation and leisure programs available and accessible? _____

2. Are financial resources available for accessing home and community recreation and leisure opportunities?

_____

_____

3. Is transportation to recreation and leisure opportunities available? _____

4. Is supported recreation and leisure available? _____

Source: Transition Planning Inventory, by G. Clark and J. R. Patton, 1998, Austin, TX: PRO-ED. Copyright 1998 by PRO-ED, Inc. Reprinted with permission.

Community Participation

COMMUNITY ASSESSMENT

Dates of Assessment: _____ Compiled by: _____

Identification Information

A. **Name** _____

B. **Address** _____

_____

C. **Community** _____

Information on Local Businesses/Employment Opportunities

List examples of businesses within a 1-mile radius of the student's home.

List examples of businesses within a 5-mile radius of the student's home.

List examples of entry-level job openings advertised in local newspapers.

List other sources of job leads available in this community (e.g., job boards in shopping centers or supermarkets, Department of Economic and Employment Development offices, radio or television bulletin boards).

Transportation Information

What type of transportation is available to the student from his or her home?

A. **Public Transportation**

(If public transportation is available, please attach appropriate schedule).

Bus   YES   NO   Line number _____

Subway   YES   NO   Line number _____

Light Rail   YES   NO   Line number _____

B. **Specialized Transportation**

Specialized Public Bus   YES   NO

How does the student access the service? _____

_____

_____

Specialized Public Van   YES   NO

How does the student access the service? _____

_____

_____

C. Taxi Service   YES   NO

List taxi companies and telephone numbers:

    Company   Telephone Number

    _____   _____

    _____   _____

    _____   _____

D. Other Transportation Services

List other transportation services and how they are accessed (e.g., voucher programs for taxis, vans, or car pool services through the Department of Aging):

Community Resources

What community resources are available in the student's community?

A. Recreational Resources

List organizations and recreational services available in the student's community.

B. Religious Resources

List organizations and religious services available in the student's community.

C. Consumer Resources

List organizations and services available to consumers in the student's community.

(continues)

Human Resources

A. Service Agencies

Public Service Agencies. List the federal, state, or local agencies that provide service in the student's community (e.g., Department of Health, Social Services).

Private Service Agencies. List the private agencies that provide service in the student's community (e.g., Catholic or Jewish Charities, Red Cross).

Adult Service Resources

A. Employment Training Resources

Public Service Agencies. List the federal, state, or local agencies that provide employment training in the student's community (e.g., Department of Economic & Employment Development, Division of Rehabilitation Services).

Private Service Agencies. List the private agencies that provide employment training in the student's community (e.g., Association for Retarded Citizens, Catholic Charities).

B. Residential Services

Public Service Agencies. List the federal, state, or local agencies that provide residential services in the student's community (e.g., Department of Social Services, Department of Housing).

Private Service Agencies. List the private agencies that provide residential services in the student's community (e.g., Association for Retarded Citizens, Jewish Charities, Y.M.C.A.).

C. Day Programming and Sheltered Employment Services

Public Service Agencies. List the federal, state, or local agencies that provide day programming and sheltered employment in the student's community (e.g., Division of Rehabilitation Services).

Private Service Agencies. List the private agencies that provide day programming and sheltered employment in the student's community (e.g., Association for Retarded Citizens, Centers for the Handicapped).

Source: Assess for Success: Handbook on Transition Assessment, by P. L. Sitlington, D. A. Neubert, W. Begun, R. C. Lombard, and P. J. Leconte, 1996, Reston, VA: The Council for Exceptional Children. Copyright 1996 by the Council for Exceptional Children. Reprinted with permission.

Health

Name: _____ Date: _____

Transition Health Care Assessment

The adolescent demonstrates knowledge of his/her health condition and its management by:

1. Being able to explain the etiology and pathophysiology underlying his/her medical condition.	Yes	No	N/A
2. Describing long-term management and treatment regimen.	Yes	No	N/A
3. Identifying actual or potential problems in adhering to treatment.	Yes	No	N/A
4. Describing the use of prescribed medications.	Yes	No	N/A
5. Stating the normal and abnormal pertinent laboratory values and diagnostic test results and their meaning.	Yes	No	N/A

Adolescent engages in preventative health behaviors by:

1. Keeping appointment with a Primary Care Physician (PCP).	Yes	No	N/A
2. Being current with immunizations and health care screenings.	Yes	No	N/A
3. Abstaining from using alcohol, cigarettes, and drugs, and having unprotected sex.	Yes	No	N/A
4. Taking adequate measures for self-protection such as wearing orthotics.	Yes	No	N/A
5. Wearing Medi-Alert bracelet/necklace.	Yes	No	N/A
6. Engaging in some form of regular exercise.	Yes	No	N/A
7. Visiting dentist on a regular basis.	Yes	No	N/A
8. Maintaining an oral hygiene program of brushing and flossing teeth.	Yes	No	N/A
9. Recognizing early signs and symptoms of infections (URI, UTI).	Yes	No	N/A

Adolescent demonstrates knowledge of emergency measures by:

1. Having reliable phone access at home.	Yes	No	N/A
2. Keeping list of phone numbers of family and friends to call in urgent/emergency situations/matters.	Yes	No	N/A
3. Keeping list of phone numbers of health and nonhealth emergency services, poison control center.	Yes	No	N/A
4. Identifying the location of the nearest ER.	Yes	No	N/A
5. Notifying the fire department of special needs and reviewing their emergency evacuations.	Yes	No	N/A
6. Notifying utility companies of additional service needs.	Yes	No	N/A

Adolescent demonstrates understanding of his/her need for environmental modifications/accommodations by:

1. Having electrical modifications done for life support equipment (ventilator) or other durable equipment such as hover lift.	Yes	No	N/A
2. Securing storage space for supplies and equipment.	Yes	No	N/A
3. Having wheelchair ramps and modifications made for doors, tubs.	Yes	No	N/A
4. Disposing of supplies (e.g., needles) properly and safely.	Yes	No	N/A

Adolescent demonstrates the ability to monitor his/her health condition by:

1. Knowing when to seek medical care.	Yes	No	N/A
2. Identifying triggers for problems or flare-ups of medical condition.	Yes	No	N/A
3. Being able to describe environmental risks affecting his/her medical condition (increased elevations, large crowds, airport scanners).	Yes	No	N/A

Adolescent demonstrates ability to manage his/her special health care needs by:

1. Keeping appointments with specialty care provider(s).	Yes	No	N/A
2. Knowing when to order medications and supplies.	Yes	No	N/A
3. Knowing when to replace durable equipment.	Yes	No	N/A
4. Keeping extra/backup supplies or equipment.	Yes	No	N/A
5. Demonstrating ability to manage attendant(s), home health aide(s), school aide(s), and interpreter(s).	Yes	No	N/A
6. Demonstrating ability to hire and use personal attendants/assistants (PAS).	Yes	No	N/A

Adolescent demonstrates ability to communicate effectively by:

1. Seeking answers to health-related concerns.	Yes	No	N/A
2. Being able to ask questions of providers.	Yes	No	N/A
3. Obtaining appropriate communication devices/systems as needed.	Yes	No	N/A
4. Making contact with teen/young adult support groups/camps.	Yes	No	N/A

Adolescent demonstrates ability to access community resources by:

1. Locating resources in the community.	Yes	No	N/A
2. Demonstrating ability to access community resources.	Yes	No	N/A
3. Accessing community transportation as need arises.	Yes	No	N/A
4. Providing school nurse with relevant health care information such as medication schedule during school hours, necessary treatments, and conditions that require monitoring.	Yes	No	N/A

(continues)

Adolescent demonstrates responsible sexual activity by:

1. Identifying high-risk situations for exploitation and victimization. Yes No N/A

2. Being able to provide reliable sexual history (e.g., nature/level of sexual activity, previous pregnancies, number of partners, STDs, exposure to HIV). Yes No N/A

3. Describing how an STD affects and is affected by the chronic condition. Yes No N/A

4. Using contraception/STD prevention strategies. Yes No N/A

Adolescent demonstrates knowledge of need to obtain information and reproductive counseling by:

1. Knowing when to seek reproductive counseling. Yes No N/A

2. Understanding the implications of pregnancy and timing of pregnancy in terms of age. Yes No N/A

3. Considering the realistic challenges of becoming a parent. Yes No N/A

Adolescent demonstrates ability to keep track of health records by:

1. Having copy of health records. Yes No N/A

2. Ensuring adult provider has health records. Yes No N/A

3. Having insurance card or copy. Yes No N/A

4. Recording and keeping appointments for medical visits, dental care, and so on. Yes No N/A

Adolescent demonstrates knowledge of health insurance concerns and issues by:

1. Identifying when eligibility terminates for health insurance coverage. Yes No N/A

2. Budgeting or making arrangements for medically related expenses not covered by third party payer. Yes No N/A

3. Applying for income assistance (SSI) and public financed health services. Yes No N/A

Adolescent demonstrates knowledge of his/her accommodations as specified by law by:

1. Identifying need for school/work setting accommodations. Yes No N/A

2. Contacting the college/university Office of Disabled Students. Yes No N/A

3. Being able to describe rights as specified in Americans with Disabilities Act. Yes No N/A

4. Accessing other community based agencies for services (e.g., social service, vocational rehabilitation). Yes No N/A

Adolescent demonstrates ability to use transportation safely by:

1. Recognizing the limitations of driver's license and ability to drive.	Yes	No	N/A
2. Knowing how to take bus, train, or other mode of public transportation.	Yes	No	N/A
3. Reading bus or other mode of transportation travel schedule.	Yes	No	N/A
4. Having the correct/sufficient amount of money for fare, pass, or auto usage.	Yes	No	N/A
5. Knowing the destination address, phone number, and general direction of where it is located.	Yes	No	N/A
6. Knowing etiquette according to mode of transportation (e.g., waiting one's turn, getting up for elderly).	Yes	No	N/A
7. Being knowledgeable of and able to access local transportation (e.g., Dial-A-Ride, Access Van).	Yes	No	N/A
8. Being aware of safety concerns in traveling neighborhood and community routes.	Yes	No	N/A
9. Knowing length of travel time required and how it will impact scheduling of the day's activities (e.g., when it will get dark, getting back in time for meals).	Yes	No	N/A
10. Knowing to avoid sitting next to passengers with colds, cough, and so on.	Yes	No	N/A
11. Being able to identify appropriate protective behaviors/interactions with strangers.	Yes	No	N/A
12. Carrying phone number of trusted individuals (friends/family) who can provide assistance if needed (e.g., missing last bus of day).	Yes	No	N/A
13. Always informing trusted individual(s) of where he or she is going and time of return.	Yes	No	N/A

Name: _____ Date: _____

Getting To Know Your Anger

Anger is a normal, human emotion. *It is intense.* Everyone gets angry and has a right to his or her anger. The trick is managing your anger effectively so that it will move you in POSITIVE, not negative, directions.

The first step in **ANGER MANAGEMENT** is to get to know your anger by recognizing its symptoms.

DO YOU . . .

___ physical	___ emotional	___ behavioral
____ grit your teeth?	____ feel like running away?	____ cry/yell/scream?
____ get a headache?	____ get depressed?	____ use substances?
____ get sweaty palms?	____ feel guilty?	____ get sarcastic?
____ get dizzy?	____ feel resentment?	____ lose sense of humor?
____ get red-faced?	____ become anxious?	____ become abusive?
____ get a stomachache?	____ feel like lashing out?	____ withdraw?
____ _____	____ _____	____ _____
____ _____	____ _____	____ _____

DOES YOUR ANGER . . .

____ last too long?   ____ make you feel ill?
____ become too intense?   ____ come too frequently?
____ lead to aggression?   ____ flare up too quickly?
____ hurt relationships?   ____ _____
____ prevent you from doing your work at home or at school?   ____ _____
____ creep out in mysterious ways?   ____ _____

ANGER INVENTORY (Rate 1–5) Rank your anger in the following situations.

    1—no annoyance   2—little irritated   3—upset   4—quite angry   5—very angry

____ You've overheard people joking about you, your family, or your friends.

____ You're not being treated with respect or consideration.

____ You're singled out for corrections while the actions of others go unnoticed.

____ You're hounded by a salesperson from the moment you walk into a store.

____ You're trying to discuss something important with someone who isn't giving you a chance to talk or express your feelings.

____ Someone offers continual, unsolicited advice.

____ You're in a discussion with someone who persists in arguing about a topic he or she knows very little about.

____ You've had a busy day and your parents/guardians greet you with complaints about what you haven't finished.

____ Someone is given special consideration because of his or her popularity, good looks, financial position, or family status.

____ Someone comments on your being overweight/underweight.

____ **TOTAL**

Additional situations that spark YOUR anger.

_____
_____
_____

. . . perhaps it's time to work on your anger management skills!

Source: Life Management Skills II, by Wellness Reproductions and Publishing, Inc., 1993, Beachwood, OH: Author. Copyright 1993 by Wellness Reproductions and Publishing, Inc. Reprinted with permission.

Name: _____ Date: _____

Sexuality Assessment

Body Parts and Function
_____ Knows that some body parts are private and should not be displayed in public.
_____ Can distinguish between private versus public behavior and information.
_____ Knows how to appropriately control sexual drive.
_____ Knows that certain personal activities are to take place in private (e.g., toileting, masturbation).
_____ Knows normalcy and health of both male and female genitalia.
_____ Knowledgeable of the human life cycle and the changes that the body undergoes through time.

Personal Relationships
_____ Knowledgeable of the concept of dating.
_____ Knowledgeable of the concepts of marriage and divorce.
_____ Knowledgeable of the concepts of heterosexual, homosexual, monogamous, and bigamous relationships.
_____ Knowledgeable of the concept of abstinence.
_____ Knowledgeable of safer sex practices.

Personal Rights and Responsibilities
_____ Knows that whether or not to engage in sexual activity is a choice that one decides.
_____ Knows that he or she decides whether or not someone else may touch him or her.
_____ Can respect another's right to not be touched.
_____ Knows personal limits and boundaries in a relationship.

Sexual Abuse
_____ Knowledgeable of the concept of rape and date rape, how to prevent it, and how to report it.
_____ Knowledgeable of sexual abuse and exploitation.
_____ Can identify the signs of sexual abuse.
_____ Knowledgeable of the concept of sexual harassment.
_____ Knowledgeable of the emotional and psychological impact of rape, sexual abuse, and sexual harassment.
_____ Knows how to report sexual abuse, rape, and sexual harassment, and can identify a person or place to go for assistance.

Sexually Transmitted Diseases
_____ Knowledgeable of the concept, causes, and ramifications of sexually transmitted diseases, including HIV and AIDS.
_____ Knowledgeable of the signs and symptoms of sexually transmitted diseases, including HIV and AIDS.

_____ Other:
_____ Other:

Identified Areas of Need:

1.

2.

3.

Self-Determination

Name: _____ Date: _____

Self-Determination/Self-Advocacy Checklist

How well do you know yourself? How well do you know what you like or prefer for yourself? How well do you know what you value as important in your life and how those values affect your decisions? How well can you tell others about yourself—your strengths and weaknesses? How well can you tell others how they can be supportive and helpful to you when you need help? How well can you look at your life and make changes when you see things you want to change?

The checklist below will help you know yourself better in these areas. Answer as honestly as you can. If you don't know, you may say that you don't know by checking DK.

Descriptions of Me	School		Home/Community		
	Yes	No	Yes	No	DK
I can describe my strengths.	☐	☐	☐	☐	☐
I can describe my weaknesses.	☐	☐	☐	☐	☐
I can explain my disability label.	☐	☐	☐	☐	☐
I can explain what I need from special education services.	☐	☐	☐	☐	☐
I can explain how I learn best.	☐	☐	☐	☐	☐
I can explain what does not help in learning.	☐	☐	☐	☐	☐
I know my interests.	☐	☐	☐	☐	☐
I know my values.	☐	☐	☐	☐	☐
I can ask for help without getting upset.	☐	☐	☐	☐	☐
I can state what I want to learn.	☐	☐	☐	☐	☐
I can state what I want to do when I graduate.	☐	☐	☐	☐	☐
I can state my rights as a person with a disability.	☐	☐	☐	☐	☐
I speak confidently and with eye contact when talking with others.	☐	☐	☐	☐	☐
I can tell teachers or work supervisors what I need to be able to do my work.	☐	☐	☐	☐	☐
I know how to look for support or help.	☐	☐	☐	☐	☐
I know how to set goals for myself.	☐	☐	☐	☐	☐
I know how to get information to make decisions.	☐	☐	☐	☐	☐
I can solve problems that come up in my life.	☐	☐	☐	☐	☐
I can develop a plan of action for goals.	☐	☐	☐	☐	☐
I can begin my work on time.	☐	☐	☐	☐	☐
I can stay on a work schedule or time plan.	☐	☐	☐	☐	☐
I can work independently.	☐	☐	☐	☐	☐
I can manage my time to stay on tasks until they are done.	☐	☐	☐	☐	☐
I can compare my work to a standard and evaluate its quality.	☐	☐	☐	☐	☐
I can tell when my plan of action is working or not.	☐	☐	☐	☐	☐
I can change goals or my plan of action.	☐	☐	☐	☐	☐

Source: Transition Planning Inventory, by G. Clark and J. R. Patton, 1998, Austin: TX: PRO-ED. Copyright 1998 by PRO-ED, Inc. Reprinted with permission.

Name: _____ Date: _____

Setting Objectives for Success Worksheet

Directions to Counselees: Choose an area of school performance that you would like to improve. Write the name of that class or area in the blank in Item 1. Finish filling in the blanks for items 1 through 6. Your peer counselor will help. When you finish, you will have set an objective for greater success in school.

Directions to Counselors: Help your student set a realistic goal for success. If a student is failing math halfway through the quarter, for example, it may be unrealistic for him/her to try to earn an A or B. Also, make sure the checkback time in Item 6 is soon enough for you to keep a close check on progress toward the goal you've set together. When finished, show this worksheet to your adult supervisor.

1. Describe the successful _____ student. List the exact behaviors a successful student does in that class or performance area.

   a. _____ b. _____
   c. _____ d. _____
   e. _____ f. _____

2. Sort and write down three behaviors that would personally help you be more success-ful. Choose the most important one for you and mark it with an (*).

   _____

   _____

   _____

3. Write an objective for the starred item. The objective must be a goal that you can do and that you can measure.

   _____

   _____

   _____

4. Test your objective. Finish this sentence by filling in your objective on the line follow-ing; "Let me show you how I can

   _____

   _____

   Can your peer counselor see you do it?
   _____ Yes
   _____ No

(continues)

5. List the exact behaviors involved in reaching that objective.

_____

_____

_____

6. Set a checkback time when you will check your progress with your peer counselor. Write that time here.

_____

Source: The Peer Counseling Training Course, by M. Phillips, revised and expanded by J. Sturkie, 1992, San Jose, CA: Resource Publications, Inc. Copyright 1992 by Resource Publications, Inc. Reprinted with permission.

Name: _____ Date: _____

Personal and Professional Goals Worksheet

Questions	Responses
1. Make a list of your dreams and aspirations. What do you want to do, have, and be?	
2. What do you most want to commit to? What are you excited about? What will give you the most satisfaction? Select your three most important goals.	
3. What short-term objectives do you need to reach your long-term goals?	
4. What resources (friends, colleagues, training opportunities, materials) can you use to help reach those goals?	
5. When do you expect to achieve your goals?	
6. What changes will you have to make to achieve your goals?	
7. What are the potential barriers that will prevent you from reaching your goals?	
8. Where can you place your goals calendar so that it is a visible reminder?	

Source: "Juggling Roles and Making Changes," by J. L. Luckner, Winter 1996, *Teaching Exceptional Children*, p. 27. Copyright 1996 by the Council For Exceptional Children. Reprinted with permission.

Communication

Communication Summary Form

Directions:
Complete this form by reviewing the student's records and interviewing the student's parents, peers, teachers, and speech–language pathologist.

Name of student: _____

Date last revised: _____   _____   _____

Unaided Systems	Responds to receptively		Uses expressively		If yes, describe special instructions/procedures
Nonsymbolic behaviors*					
Vocalizations	Y	N	Y	N	_____
Affect	Y	N	Y	N	_____
Body movement	Y	N	Y	N	_____
Gestural	Y	N	Y	N	_____
Physiological	Y	N	Y	N	_____
Visual	Y	N	Y	N	_____
Symbolic behaviors*					
Gestures	Y	N	Y	N	_____
Sign language	Y	N	Y	N	_____
Speech	Y	N	Y	N	_____
Pictures	Y	N	Y	N	_____
Printed word	Y	N	Y	N	_____
Braille	Y	N	Y	N	_____

Communication Summary Form *(Continued)*

Aided Systems	Responds to receptively		Uses expressively		If yes, describe special instructions/procedures
Nonelectronic devices*					
Single-sheet	Y	N	Y	N	_____
Multiple-sheets	Y	N	Y	N	_____
Electronic devices*					
Tape recorder	Y	N	Y	N	_____
Personal computer	Y	N	Y	N	_____
Dedicated aids (e.g., Touch Talker, Wolf, or SpeechPac)	Y	N	Y	N	_____
_____	Y	N	Y	N	_____
_____	Y	N	Y	N	_____
Vocabulary displays*					
Objects	Y	N	Y	N	_____
Photographs	Y	N	Y	N	_____
Line drawings	Y	N	Y	N	_____
Symbols	Y	N	Y	N	_____
Printed words	Y	N	Y	N	_____
Brailled	Y	N	Y	N	_____
Methods of using the devices					
Direct selection	Y	N	Y	N	_____
Scanning	Y	N	Y	N	_____

_____

*Attach vocabulary lists or sample overlays from communication devices.

Source: Student Portfolio: A System for Documenting the Strengths, Needs, and Abilities of Students Who Are Deaf–Blind, by Kansas State Board of Education, 1996, Topeka, KS: Author. Copyright 1996 by the Kansas State Board of Education. Reprinted with permission.

Name: _____ Date: _____

Reading Style Preference Checklist

To complete this checklist, please read through all statements below. Then go back through them again and check off the statements that sound most like you.

How I Learn Best

_____ I learn best by reading silently.

_____ I learn best by reading out loud to myself.

_____ I learn best by reading out loud in a small group.

_____ I learn best by having someone read to me.

_____ I learn best by listening to a tape recording.

_____ I learn best by listening to a tape recording and following along in the reading.

_____ I learn best by discussing what I read.

Types of Reading Problems I Face

_____ I often don't understand what I have just read.

_____ I often don't remember what I have just read.

_____ I have trouble with new vocabulary.

_____ I always feel that I need extra time to complete reading assignments.

_____ I have trouble concentrating when I read.

_____ I get tired easily when I read.

_____ I often lose my place when I read.

_____ I skip words or lines when I read.

Name: _____ Date: _____

Writing Self-Assessment: Skills and Attitudes

Part I: Please complete the following statements by placing the number from 1 through 5 that best reflects *your* assessment of your skills. (Using a scale 1 through 5, 1 indicates the best.)

I would rate my reading skills. # _____
  (Choose 1 through 5, 1 being the best.)

I would rate my knowledge of grammar. # _____

I would rate my writing skills. # _____

I would rate my library research skills. # _____

I would rate my skills on the word processor. # _____

What I want most to improve about my writing this semester is _____
_____.

Part II: Please complete the following sentences:

When I am asked to read a book, I feel _____
_____.

When I am asked to write a paper for school, I feel _____
_____.

When I am asked to write my paper on a word processor, I feel _____
_____.

I know my paper is good when _____
_____.

When a teacher grades my paper, I feel _____
_____.

When I am asked to grade my own paper, I feel _____
_____.

Source: "Teaching Writing to College Students with Learning Disabilities," by J. R. Pardes and R. Z. Rich, 1996, *Intervention in School and Clinic, 31*(5), p. 300. Copyright 1996 by PRO-ED, Inc. Reprinted with permission.

Student: _____ Date: _____

Assistive Technology Needs Inventory— Communications Application

Directions: Describe each specific need as a function of each adult setting.

	Workplace	Education	Home	Community
Reading				
computer				
optical character recognition				
text enhancement				
tape recorder				
page turners				
electronic books				
Writing				
computer				
specialized software:				
word processing				
spell check				
grammar check				
speech recognition				
outlining				
brainstorming				
alternative keyboard				
adapted grips (pen)				
adapted paper				
slant board				
Speaking				
speech synthesis				
Listening				
assistive listening device (e.g., FM)				
tape recorder				

Interpersonal Relationships

School and Community Social Skills Rating Checklist

Student's Name: _____   Birthdate: _____

Sex: _____ Male   _____ Female   Date: _____

School: _____   Rater: _____

Current grade level or class assignment: _____   Special education classification: _____

DIRECTIONS: Check each item that describes the student.

CLASSROOM RELATED BEHAVIORS

The student adequately and appropriately:

- [ ] 1. attends to teacher during instruction.
- [ ] 2. maintains correct sitting posture.
- [ ] 3. gains the teacher's attention.
- [ ] 4. answers questions asked by teachers.
- [ ] 5. asks teacher for assistance or information.
- [ ] 6. shares materials with classmates.
- [ ] 7. keeps own desk in order.
- [ ] 8. enters class without disruption.
- [ ] 9. follows classroom rules.
- [ ] 10. cooperates with work partners.
- [ ] 11. ignores distractions.
- [ ] 12. stays on task during seatwork.
- [ ] 13. completes work on time.
- [ ] 14. participates politely in classroom discussion.
- [ ] 15. makes relevant remarks during classroom discussion.
- [ ] 16. follows verbal directions.
- [ ] 17. follows written directions.
- [ ] 18. speaks politely about schoolwork.
- [ ] 19. participates in classroom introductions.
- [ ] 20. completes homework on time.
- [ ] 21. uses free time in class productively.

SCHOOL BUILDING RELATED BEHAVIORS

The student adequately and appropriately:

- [ ] 22. follows procedures for boarding school bus.
- [ ] 23. follows bus riding rules.

School and Community Social Skills Rating Checklist (Continued)

☐ 24. walks through hallways and passes to class.

☐ 25. waits in lines.

☐ 26. uses rest room facilities.

☐ 27. uses drinking fountain.

☐ 28. follows lunchroom rules.

☐ 29. uses table manners.

☐ 30. responds to school authorities.

☐ 31. deals with accusations at school.

PERSONAL SKILLS

The student adequately and appropriately:

☐ 32. says "please" and "thank you."

☐ 33. speaks in tone of voice for the situation.

☐ 34. takes turns in games and activities.

☐ 35. tells the truth.

☐ 36. accepts consequences for wrong doing.

☐ 37. maintains grooming.

☐ 38. avoids inappropriate physical contact.

☐ 39. exhibits hygienic behavior.

☐ 40. expresses enthusiasm.

☐ 41. makes positive statements about self.

☐ 42. expresses anger in nonaggressive ways.

☐ 43. accepts praise.

☐ 44. stays out of fights.

☐ 45. deals with embarrassment.

☐ 46. chooses clothing for social events.

☐ 47. deals with failure.

☐ 48. deals with being left out.

INTERACTION INITIATIVE SKILLS

The student adequately and appropriately:

☐ 49. greets peers.

☐ 50. borrows from peers.

☐ 51. asks other children to play.

(continues)

School and Community Social Skills Rating Checklist *(Continued)*

- [ ] 52. expresses sympathy.
- [ ] 53. asks peers for help.
- [ ] 54. makes invitations.
- [ ] 55. introduces self.
- [ ] 56. makes introductions.
- [ ] 57. initiates conversations.
- [ ] 58. joins activities with peers.
- [ ] 59. congratulates peers and adults.
- [ ] 60. makes apologies.
- [ ] 61. excuses self from groups and conversations.
- [ ] 62. expresses feelings.
- [ ] 63. expresses affection.
- [ ] 64. stands up for a friend.
- [ ] 65. asks for dates.
- [ ] 66. gives compliments.
- [ ] 67. makes complaints.

INTERACTION RESPONSE SKILLS

The student adequately and appropriately:

- [ ] 68. smiles when encountering acquaintances.
- [ ] 69. listens when another child speaks.
- [ ] 70. participates in group activities.
- [ ] 71. helps peers when asked.
- [ ] 72. accepts ideas different from own.
- [ ] 73. meets with adults.
- [ ] 74. maintains conversations.
- [ ] 75. responds to teasing and name calling.
- [ ] 76. responds to constructive criticism.
- [ ] 77. recognizes feelings of others.
- [ ] 78. respects the space of others.
- [ ] 79. responds to peer pressure.
- [ ] 80. deals with an angry person.
- [ ] 81. makes refusals.
- [ ] 82. answers complaints.

School and Community Social Skills Rating Checklist *(Continued)*

COMMUNITY RELATED SKILLS

The student adequately and appropriately:

- [ ] 83. asks for directions in public.
- [ ] 84. gives directions.
- [ ] 85. exhibits sportsmanship as a game participant.
- [ ] 86. exhibits polite behavior and sportsmanship as a spectator.
- [ ] 87. disposes of wastepaper and debris in public.
- [ ] 88. respects the rights of others in public.
- [ ] 89. respects private property.
- [ ] 90. exhibits good audience behaviors.
- [ ] 91. responds to public authority.
- [ ] 92. asserts self to gain service.
- [ ] 93. deals with public officials over the phone.

WORK RELATED SOCIAL SKILLS

The student adequately and appropriately:

- [ ] 94. sets goals for work.
- [ ] 95. negotiates on the job.
- [ ] 96. responds to unwarranted criticism.
- [ ] 97. asks for feedback on the job.
- [ ] 98. minds own business on the job.
- [ ] 99. chooses a time for small talk.
- [ ] 100. refrains from excessive complaining.

Source: Social Skills for School and Community (pp. 269–273), by L. R. Sargent, 1991, Reston, VA: Division of Mental Retardation, Council for Exceptional Children. Copyright 1991 by the Council for Exceptional Children. Reprinted with permission.

LET'S LOOK AT INTERPERSONAL RELATIONSHIPS

For each question, consider how you would respond in each of the four different settings. Place a check in the box when you have considered that situation.

	At Home	At School	In The Community	On The Job

Conflict

1. When a problem comes up, what do you usually do?
2. What is the best thing to do when a problem comes up?
3. When a problem comes up, what do you fear the most?
4. What are ways to cope with being afraid that work for you?
5. Who would be a good person (or place) to go to for more help when you are afraid?
6. How do you handle the stress of problems?
7. How is this working for you?
8. When a problem comes up, do you feel sad, upset, or angry?
9. What do you do when you feel sad?
10. What do you do when you feel angry?
11. What problems are you having now?
12. How are you handling these problems?
13. Do you know someone that you trust who would be a good person to go to when a problem comes up?

Friends

14. Who are your friends or people you like a lot?
15. How did you go about making these friends?
16. Do you get along well with your friends or people you like?
17. What do you like the most about these people?
18. What do you think they like most about you?

Resolution

19. What would you like to change about your social situation or interpersonal relationships?
20. Do you think these areas can change?
21. Do you know how to change these areas?
22. How motivated are you to change these areas by making changes yourself?
23. Who can you ask or where can you go for help?

Appendix A
Statement of Transition Needs

Student Name: _____ School Name: _____

DOB: _____ Age: _____ Grade: _____ Projected Year of Graduation: _____ IEP/ITP Date: _____

                                                                    Statement of Transition Needs

Employment

1. Knows job requirements and demands.   _____

2. Makes informed choices among occupational
   alternatives.   _____

3. Knows how to get a job.   _____

4. Demonstrates general job skills and work attitudes.   _____

5. Has the specific job skills.   _____

Further Education/Training

6. Knows how to gain entry into a community employment training program.   _____

7. Knows how to gain entry into a GED program.   _____

8. Knows how to gain entry into a vocational/technical
   school.   _____

9. Knows how to gain entry into a college or university.   _____

10. Can succeed in a postsecondary program.   _____

Daily Living

11. Maintains personal grooming and hygiene. _____

12. Knows how to locate a place to live. _____

13. Knows how to set up living arrangements. _____

14. Performs everyday household tasks. _____

15. Manages own money. _____

16. Uses local transportation systems. _____

Leisure Activities

17. Performs indoor leisure activities. _____

18. Performs outdoor leisure activities. _____

19. Uses settings that provide entertainment. _____

Community Participation

20. Knows his or her basic legal rights. _____

21. Participates as an active citizen. _____

22. Makes legal decisions affecting his or her life. _____

23. Locates community services and resources. _____

24. Uses services and resources successfully. _____

25. Knows how to obtain financial services. _____

Health

26. Maintains good physical health. _____

27. Addresses physical problems. _____

28. Maintains good mental health. _____

29. Addresses mental health problems. _____

30. Knows how the reproductive system works. _____

31. Makes informed choices regarding sexual behavior. _____

Self-Determination

32. Recognizes and accepts own strengths and limitations. _____

33. Expresses feelings and ideas appropriately. _____

34. Expresses feelings and ideas to others confidently. _____

35. Sets personal goals.   _____

36. Makes personal decisions.   _____

Communication

37. Has needed speaking skills.   _____

38. Has needed listening skills.   _____

39. Has needed reading skills.   _____

40. Has needed writing skills.   _____

Interpersonal Relationships

41. Gets along well with family members.   _____

42. Knowledgeable of and possesses skills of parenting.   _____

43. Establishes and maintains friendships.   _____

44. Knowledgeable of appropriate social behavior in   _____
    a variety of settings.

45. Possesses skills for getting along with coworkers.   _____

46. Possesses skills for getting along with supervisor.   _____

Case Study: Kevin

Scenario

Kevin is a 15-year-old who has a learning disability. He has been receiving special education services since he was in elementary school. He currently is included in general education classes for most of his instructional day.

Kevin is a bright and hard-working student who wants to go to college when high school is over. This is a viable choice for him. However, he struggles with written assignments and he has difficulty with many different study skills, especially time management, note taking, and organizational skills.

His transition planning needs to focus on these areas in which he has difficulty and that are critical for success in postsecondary settings.

Sequence of Activities

1. The *Transition Planning Inventory* was completed by Kevin, his parents, and school-based personnel.

   Note: Everyone thought it would be a good idea to examine Kevin's transition needs; as a result, all three forms were completed and returned.

2. The TPI Profile, based on the responses of Kevin, his parents, and teachers, was completed (see p. 156).

Note: Kevin received low ratings for TPI Item 10 (*Can succeed in an appropriate postsecondary program*) from all three sources.

3. The Further Assessment Recommendations Form was completed (see p. 157).

   Note: All parties agreed that further assessment was needed in relation to Kevin's ability to deal successfully with the demands of college coursework.

4. The expanded list of competencies for Item 10 was completed from the Comprehensive Informal Inventory of Knowledge and Skills for Transition (see p. 158).

   Note: Three of the items were identified as needing goals written in the IEP/ITP. More assessment of the study skills area was suggested.

5. The Study Skills Inventory (SSI) was administered to Kevin by his teacher (see p. 159–161).

   Note: The results of the SSI clarify the areas where instructional goals need to be written and instruction provided. Furthermore, linkage goals need to be generated to ensure that Kevin continues to receive attention for his study skills needs when he is at college.

KEVIN

Section V. Profile

Planning Areas	School Rating	Home Rating	Student Rating	Knowledge/Skills Goals	Linkage Goals
	Strongly Disagree ← NA 0 1 2 3 4 5 DK → Strongly Agree	Strongly Disagree ← NA 0 1 2 3 4 5 DK → Strongly Agree	Strongly Disagree ← NA 0 1 2 3 4 5 DK → Strongly Agree		
EMPLOYMENT					
1. knows job requirements and demands	NA 0 1 2 ③ 4 5 DK	NA 0 1 2 3 ④ 5 DK	NA 0 1 ② 3 4 5 DK		
2. makes informed choices	NA 0 1 2 ③ 4 5 DK	NA 0 1 2 ③ 4 5 DK	NA 0 1 2 3 ④ 5 DK		
3. knows how to get a job	NA 0 1 2 3 ④ 5 DK	NA 0 1 2 ③ 4 5 DK	NA 0 1 2 3 ④ 5 DK		
4. demonstrates general job skills and work attitude	NA 0 1 2 ③ 4 5 DK	NA 0 1 2 3 ④ 5 DK	NA 0 1 2 3 4 ⑤ DK		
5. has specific job skills	ⓃⒶ 0 1 2 3 4 5 DK	NA 0 1 2 3 4 5 ⒹⓀ	ⓃⒶ 0 1 2 3 4 5 DK		
FURTHER EDUCATION/TRAINING					
6. knows how to gain entry into community employment training	ⓃⒶ 0 1 2 3 4 5 DK	ⓃⒶ 0 1 2 3 4 5 DK	ⓃⒶ 0 1 2 3 4 5 DK		
7. knows how to gain entry into GED program	ⓃⒶ 0 1 2 3 4 5 DK	ⓃⒶ 0 1 2 3 4 5 DK	ⓃⒶ 0 1 2 3 4 5 DK		
8. knows how to gain entry into vocational/technical school	ⓃⒶ 0 1 2 3 4 5 DK	ⓃⒶ 0 1 2 3 4 5 DK	ⓃⒶ 0 1 2 3 4 5 DK		
9. knows how to gain entry into college or university	NA 0 1 2 3 ④ 5 DK	NA 0 1 ② 3 4 5 DK	NA 0 1 2 ③ 4 5 DK		
10. can succeed in a postsecondary program	NA ⓪ 1 2 3 4 5 DK	NA 0 1 ② 3 4 5 DK	NA ⓪ 1 2 3 4 5 DK		

 **KEVIN**

Section VI. Further Assessment Recommendations									
	Specific Transition Needs								
Type of Assessment	Study Skills								
• **Observations**									
• **Interviews**									
• **Checklists/Rating Scales**									
• **Curriculum-Based Assessments**									
• **Functional Vocational Evaluation**									
• **Standardized or Nonstandardized Tests or Inventories:**									
Study Skills Inventory (Level 3)	✓								
• **Medical Examination**									
• **Hearing Evaluation**									
• **Vision Evaluation**									
• **Speech–Language Evaluation**									
• **Assistive Technology Evaluation**									
• **Other:**									
Comprehensive Informal Inventory (Level 2)	✓								

KEVIN

Goals/ Objectives Needed	Further Assessment Needed	FURTHER EDUCATION/TRAINING	Notes
		10. Can succeed in an appropriate postsecondary program.	
☑	☑	Can use the academic support skills (e.g., organizational skills, time management, and other study skills) necessary to succeed in a given postsecondary setting.	_Study Skills Inventory_
☐	☐	Can perform reading skills required in the program.	
☑	☐	Can perform writing skills required in the program.	
☐	☐	Can perform math skills required in the program.	
☐	☐	Can analyze information and draw conclusions.	
☐	☐	Can manage finances.	
☑	☐	Knows how to balance priorities between classes, work, home duties, and leisure time.	
☐	☐	Knows how to use disability support services.	
☐	☐	Knows how to develop a social support system.	
☐	☐	Knows how to assess (with others) what types of support/modifications are needed.	
☐	☐	Knows how to appropriately meet with instructor (or professor) to discuss and advocate for reasonable accommodations (e.g., manner of presentation, timeliness, knowledge of necessary reasonable accommodations).	
☐	☐	Knows how to develop and implement a plan and a time line for completion of postsecondary training program.	

KEVIN

Study Skills Inventory

Completed by: _TJP_____   Student: _Kevin M._____   Date: _2/23/00_

Place the appropriate number (1, 2, or 3) in the box next to each study skill subskill (1 = Mastered—regular, appropriate use of skill; 2 = Partially Mastered—needs some improvement; 3 = Not Mastered—infrequent use of skill).

Reading Rate

- [3] Skimming
- [2] Scanning
- [2] Rapid reading
- [1] Normal rate
- [2] Study or careful reading
- [2] Understands importance of reading rates

Listening

- [1] Attends to listening activities
- [1] Applies meaning to verbal messages
- [1] Filters out auditory distractions
- [2] Comprehends verbal messages
- [1] Understands importance of listening skills

Note Taking/Outlining

- [2] Uses headings/subheadings appropriately
- [3] Takes brief and clear notes
- [3] Records essential information
- [2] Applies skill during writing activities
- [3] Uses skill during lectures

- [3] Develops organized outlines
- [2] Follows consistent notetaking format
- [1] Understands importance of note taking
- [2] Understands importance of outlining

Report Writing

- [3] Organizes thoughts in writing
- [2] Completes written reports from outline
- [2] Includes only necessary information
- [2] Uses proper sentence structure
- [1] Uses proper punctuation
- [2] Uses proper grammar and spelling
- [3] Proofreads written assignments
- [1] States clear introductory statement
- [2] Includes clear concluding statements
- [1] Understands importance of writing reports

Oral Presentations

- [1] Freely participates in oral presentations

159

KEVIN

2 Oral presentations are well organized

1 Uses gestures appropriately

1 Speaks clearly

1 Uses proper language when reporting orally

1 Understands importance of oral reporting

Graphic Aids

2 Attends to relevant elements in visual material

3 Uses visuals appropriately in presentations

3 Develops own graphic material

2 Is not confused or distracted by visual material in presentations

1 Understands importance of visual material

Test Taking

3 Studies for tests in an organized way

3 Spends appropriate amount of time studying different topics covered on a test

3 Avoids cramming for tests

3 Organizes narrative responses appropriately

2 Reads and understands directions before answering questions

3 Proofreads responses and checks for errors

3 Identifies and uses clue words in questions

2 Properly records answers

2 Saves difficult items until last

3 Eliminates obvious wrong answers

3 Systematically reviews completed tests to determine test-taking or test-studying errors

3 Corrects previous test-taking errors

1 Understands importance of test-taking skills

Library Usage

2 Uses cataloging system (card or computerized) effectively

3 Able to locate library materials

2 Understands organizational layout of library

3 Understands and uses services of media specialist

3 Understands overall functions and purposes of a library

2 Understands importance of library usage skills

Reference Materials

2 Able to identify components of different reference materials

3 Uses guide words appropriately

3 Consults reference materials when necessary

3 Uses materials appropriately to complete assignments

KEVIN

3 Able to identify different types of reference materials and sources

2 Understands importance of reference materials

Time Management

3 Completes tasks on time

3 Plans and organizes daily activities and responsibilities effectively

3 Plans and organizes weekly and monthly schedules

3 Reorganizes priorities when necessary

3 Meets scheduled deadlines

3 Accurately perceives the amount of time required to complete tasks

3 Adjusts time allotment to complete tasks

2 Accepts responsibility for managing own time

2 Understands importance of effective time management

Self-Management

2 Monitors own behavior

2 Changes own behavior as necessary

2 Thinks before acting

2 Responsible for own behavior

1 Identifies behaviors that interfere with own learning

1 Understands importance of self-management

Summary of Study Skill Proficiency

Summarize in the chart below the number of Mastered (1), Partially Mastered (2), and Not Mastered (3) study skill subskills. The number next to each study skill represents the total number of subskills for each area.

Study Skill	M	PM	NM	Study Skill	M	PM	NM
Reading Rate–6	1	4	1	Test Taking–13	1	3	9
Listening–5	4	1		Library Usage–6		2	3
Notetaking/Outlining–9	1	4	4	Reference Materials–6		2	4
Report Writing–10	3	5	2	Time Management–9		2	7
Oral Presentations–6	5	1		Self-Management–6	2	4	
Graphic Aids–5	1	2	2				

Summary Comments:

Most areas need attention—particular emphasis needs to be given to note taking, test taking, and time management.

KEVIN

Statement of Transition Needs

Student Name: _Kevin M._ School Name: _West Hills H. S._

DOB: _2/13/XX_ Age: _15_ Grade: _10_ Projected Year of Graduation: _200X_ IEP/ITP Date: _3/17/XX_

Statement of Transition Needs

Employment

1. Knows job requirements and demands. _____

2. Makes informed choices among occupational alternatives. _____

3. Knows how to get a job. _____

4. Demonstrates general job skills and work attitudes. _____

5. Has the specific job skills. _____

Further Education/Training

6. Knows how to gain entry into a community employment training program. _____

7. Knows how to gain entry into a GED program. _____

8. Knows how to gain entry into a vocational/technical school. _____

9. Knows how to gain entry into a college or university. _____

10. Can succeed in a postsecondary program. _Needs instruction on notetaking, test taking, and time management._

162

References

Area Education Agency 4. (n.d.). *Career/transition planning forms, Area 4.* Sioux Center, IA: Author.

Aune, E. P., & Ness, J. E. (1991). *Tools for transition: Student handbook.* Circle Pines, MN: American Guidance Service.

Balser, R. M., Harvey, B. M., & Rotroff, K. L. (1996). *A student's guide to the Americans with Disabilities Act: Teacher's resource guide.* Portland: Department of Vocational Services, Maine Medical Center.

Bennett, G. K., Seashore, H. G., & Wesman, A. G. (1990). *Differential Aptitude Tests, Fifth Edition.* San Antonio: Harcourt Brace Educational Measurement.

Betz, C. L. (1998). *Transition health care assessment guide.* Los Angeles: Health and Ready to Work.

Brigance, A. H. (1995). *BRIGANCE Life Skills Inventory.* North Billerica, MA: Curriculum Associates.

Brolin, D. E. (1992). *Life-Centered Career Education (LCCE) Knowledge and Performance Batteries.* Reston, VA: Council for Exceptional Children.

Clark, G. M. (1998). *Assessment for transitions planning.* Austin, TX: PRO-ED.

Clark, G. M., & Patton, J. R. (1997). *Transition Planning Inventory.* Austin, TX: PRO-ED.

Crawford, J. (1981). *Crawford Small Parts Dexterity Test.* San Antonio: Psychological Corp.

Dowdy, C., & Evers, R. (1996). Preparing students for transition. *Intervention in School and Clinic, 31*(4), 197–208.

Dunn, R., Dunn, K., & Price, G. E. (1995). *Learning Styles Inventory.* Lawrence, KS: Price Systems.

Edyburn, D. L. (1998, May/June). Self-assessment skill checklist. *Teaching Exceptional Children,* p. 7.

Enderle, J., & Severson, S. (1997). *Enderle–Severson Transition Rating Scale–Revised.* Moorehead, MN: Practical Press.

Fremont Union High School. (1980). *A slice of life.* Sunnyvale, CA: Fremont Union School District.

Furney, K. F., Carlson, N., Lisi, D., Yuan, S., & Cravedi-Cheng, L. (1993). *Speak up for yourself.* Burlington: University of Vermont.

Halpern, A. S., Irvin, L., & Munkres, J. (1986). *Social and Prevocational Information Battery–Revised.* Monterey, CA: CTB/McGraw-Hill.

Holland, A. L. (1980). *Communicative Abilities in Daily Living.* Austin, TX: PRO-ED.

Hoover, J., & Patton, J. (1995). *Teaching students with learning problems to use study skills: A teacher's guide.* Austin, TX: PRO-ED.

Jackson, D. N. (1995). *Basic Personality Inventory.* Port Huron, MI: Sigma Assessment Systems.

Jefferson County Public Schools. (n.d.). *Connections: A transition curriculum for grades 3 through 6.* Denver, CO: Author.

Kansas State Board of Education. (1996). *Student portfolio: A system for documenting the strengths, needs, and abilities of students who are deaf–blind.* Topeka: Author.

Karlsen, B., & Gardner, E. (1986). *Adult Basic Learning Examination–Second Edition.* San Antonio: Harcourt Brace Educational Measurement.

Keith, K. D., & Schalock, R. L. (1995). *Quality of Student Life Questionnaire.* Worthington, OH: IDS.

Lambert, N., Nihira, K., & Leland, H. (1993). *AAMR Adaptive Behavior Scales–School: Second Edition.* Austin, TX: PRO-ED.

Long, T., Austin, B., & Bowen, J. (1998). *Holding the road: Student self-advocacy.* Atlanta, GA: L. A. B. Educational Press.

Luckner, J. L. (1996, Winter). Judging roles and making changes. *Teaching Exceptional Children,* pp. 24–28.

McCarney, S. B. (1989). *Transition Behavior Scale.* Columbia, OH: Hawthorne Educational Service.

National Dropout Prevention Center at Clemson University. (1995). *Assessing my multiple intelligences.* Clemson, SC: Author.

Pardes, J. R., & Rich, R. Z. (1996). Teaching writing to college students with learning disabilities. *Intervention in School and Clinic, 31*(5), 297–302.

Parker, R. (1991). *Occupational Aptitude Survey and Interest Schedule* (2nd ed.). Austin, TX: PRO-ED.

Patton, J. R., & Dunn, C. (1998). *Transition from school to young adulthood: Basic concepts and recommended practices.* Austin, TX: PRO-ED.

Patton, J. R., & Polloway, E. A. (1987). Analyzing college courses. *Academic Therapy, 22,* 273–280.

Phillips, M. (revised and expanded by Sturkie, J.). (1992). *The peer counseling training course.* San Jose, CA: Resource Publications.

Power, P. W. (2000). *A guide to vocational assessment* (3rd ed.). Austin, TX: PRO-ED.

Rehabilitation Research and Training Center on Supported Employment. (1994). *Individual supports assessment.* Richmond, VA: Rehabilitation Research and Training Center on Supported Employment, Virginia Commonwealth University, Natural Supports Transition Project.

Roessler, R. T., & Bolton, B. (1986). Work personality profile. *Vocational Evaluation and Work Adjustment Bulletin, 18*(1), 8–11.

Sargent, L. R. (1991). *Social skills for school and community.* Reston, VA: Division of Mental Retardation, Council for Exceptional Children.

Sarkees-Wircenski, M., & Wircenski, J. L. (1994). Transition planning: Developing a career portfolio for students with disabilitiess. *Career Development for Exceptional Individuals, 17*(2), 203–214.

Schalock, R. L., & Keith, K. D. (1993). *Quality of Life Questionnaire.* Worthington, OH: IDS.

Sitlington, P. L., Neubert, D. A., Begun, W., Lombard, R. C., & Leconte, P. J. (1996). *Assess for success: Handbook on transition assessment.* Reston, VA: Council for Exceptional Children.

Waintrup, M., & Kelley, P. (1999). Environmental assessment. In M. Bullis & C. Davis (Eds.), *Functional assessment in transition and rehabilitation for adolescents and adults with learning disabilities* (pp. 59–62). Austin, TX: PRO-ED.

Weaver, R., & DeLuca, J. R. (1987). *Employability/life skills assessment: Ages 14–21.* Dayton, OH: Miami Valley Special Education Center and Montgomery County Board of Education.

Wellness Reproductions and Publishing, Inc. (1993). *Life management skills II.* Beachwood, OH: Author.

Yuan, F. (1994). Moving toward self-acceptance: A course for students with learning disabilities. *Intervention in School and Clinic, 29*(5), 301–309.

About the Authors

Gary M. Clark, EdD, is a professor of special education at the University of Kansas. His professional interest in adolescents with disabilities goes back to his work as a teacher, school guidance counselor, and vocational rehabilitation counselor in Texas. He has contributed to the development of the state transition guidelines for Kansas and Utah and has been a consultant in a number of states for career development, transition programming, life skills curricula, transition assessment, and secondary special education teacher education. He is a co-author of *Career Development and Transition Education for Adolescents with Disabilities* with Oliver P. Kolstoe and of the *Transition Planning Inventory* with James R. Patton. During the 1997–98 academic year he held the Matthew J. Guglielmo Visiting Professor endowed chair at California State University at Los Angeles, teaching and providing program development assistance in the area of transition for adolescents with disabilities. Address: Gary M. Clark, Department of Special Education, 3001 Robert Dole Human Development Center, University of Kansas, Lawrence, KS 66045.

James R. Patton is currently the executive editor at PRO-ED and an adjunct associate professor at the University of Texas at Austin. He has taught students with special needs at the elementary, secondary, and postsecondary levels in Charlottesville, Virginia, Honolulu, Hawaii, and Austin, Texas. He received a BS in preprofessional studies from the University of Notre Dame and completed his graduate work at the University of Virginia. Dr. Patton's primary areas of professional activity are life skills instruction, transition assessment and planning, lifelong learning, adults with learning disabilities, and accommodating students with special needs in inclusive settings.

L. Rozelle Moulton has an MS in psychology and more than 15 years of experience working in the field of individuals with disabilities and their families. Ms. Moulton is currently pursuing a PhD in Special Education at the University of Texas at Austin. Ms. Moulton has worked with a wide variety of clients as a therapist, behavior management specialist, vocational supervisor, recreation and social specialist, and consumer advocate. Additionally, while serving as a director of a community living program, Ms. Moulton has overseen community-based residential services for adults with aggression and other behavioral concerns who were dual diagnosed with mental illness and developmental or cognitive disabilities. She has also worked as a private consultant to agencies serving adults and children with a variety of disabilities. Ms. Moulton is the co-author of an instructional material titled *Teaching Kids and Adults with Autism: Building the Framework for Lifetime Learning.* After completing her doctorate, Ms. Moulton plans to pursue research and do consulting work. Her research interests include traumatic brain injury, self-determination, developmental disabilities, transition planning, family adjustment issues, and autism.

Authors' Note

We would like to hear from you

1. If you know of an informal instrument that is practical, easy-to-use, useful for obtaining transition needs information, and suitable for inclusion in Section 3 of this resource, let us know.

   If we concur and can obtain permission to use it, we will include it in future editions of this resource. Naturally, we will cite its original source and acknowledge those who made us aware of the instrument's existence.

   Send information to: Jim Patton
   PRO-ED
   8700 Shoal Creek Blvd.
   Austin, TX 78757
   Fax: 800/397-7633

2. We would also like to hear from you if you have any comments, questions, or suggestions related to this resource or the *Transition Planning Inventory* (TPI).

   Send your comments to the address above or e-mail them to:

   gclark@ukans.edu or jrpatton@onr.com

Transition Assessment Updates

Updates on informal assessments that come to our attention after the publication of this resource along with information on transition assessment and other transition topics are available at the following Web site:

   http://www.learning4living.com